STEP-BY-STEP

RIBBON
EMBROIDERY

A CREATIVE GUIDE TO
OVER 30 DESIGNS AND PROJECTS

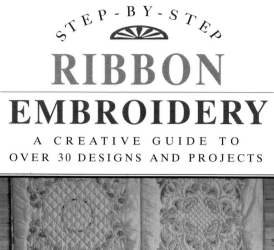

To my sister Shelley, with love

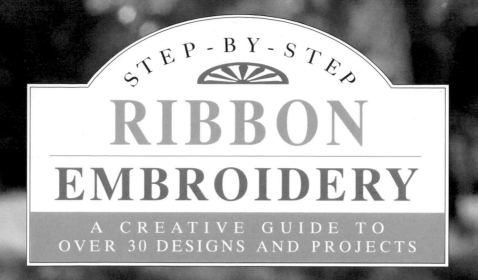

STEP-BY-STEP
RIBBON
EMBROIDERY

A CREATIVE GUIDE TO
OVER 30 DESIGNS AND PROJECTS

DI VAN NIEKERK
PHOTOGRAPHY BY CRAIG FRASER

AUTHOR'S ACKNOWLEDGEMENTS

I owe special thanks to the following people who each contributed to the writing of this book in their own way: to my husband, André, thank you once again for all your patience and support; to my two children, Ryan and Brandon, thank you for being such a pleasure to raise; to Lisah Meremetsi, without your willing help this book would never have been finished on time, and Joyce Nzimande, thank you for all your help at home; to my mother, Joan, for your exceptional skills and talented designs; to my friends Margie Horner, for helping with the baby's quilt, Gaylin Pearce, for the beautiful dress and Moira Downing for the porcelain doll.

I am indebted to Laura Milton, my editor, who moved mountains to finish this book on time. It was a pleasure working with Laura and her hard work and input was invaluable. I also thank Darren MacGurk and Petal Palmer for keeping an expert eye on matters of design and picture selection. To Linda de Villiers, thank you for having faith in me, and for your continued support. A special word of thanks must also go to Craig Fraser for his exceptional photography, and to Shelley Street for her immensely talented styling.

We are grateful, too, to the owners of the beautiful homes we used for photographic locations: Lani van Reenen of Welgelegen Guest House, Mapula and Marius Swanepoel, and Shades of Provence.

EDITOR Laura Milton
DESIGNER Darren MacGurk
COVER DESIGN Darren MacGurk
DESIGN MANAGER Petal Palmer
DESIGN ASSISTANT Dean Pollard
PHOTOGRAPHY Craig Fraser
ART DIRECTION/STYLING Shelley Street
STYLING ASSISTANT Bev de Jager
ILLUSTRATIONS Steven Felmore
DESIGN ILLUSTRATIONS Clarence Clarke

TYPESETTING Deirdré Geldenhuys, Struik DTP
REPRODUCTION Hirt & Carter (Pty) Ltd, Cape Town
PRINTING AND BINDING Tien Wah Press (Pte) Ltd, Singapore

ISBN 1 85368 542 9 (hbk)
ISBN 1 85368 703 0 (pbk)

PUBLISHER'S NOTE Imperial measurements have been adjusted or rounded up or down as appropriate to help the reader.

CONTENTS

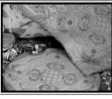

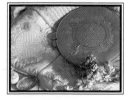

INTRODUCTION

From the moment I first glimpsed a piece of ribbon embroidery, I was fascinated by the three-dimensional effects this craft had to offer. To my mind the ribbon, when used on its own, was too restrictive and uninteresting. To 'lift' the designs, I worked on the idea of using fabric, thread and beads to complement the ribbon roses. The fabric leaves and flowers are simply glued onto the background fabric, and silk and cotton threads are used to embroider the detail. This combination creates a balanced look and adds a soft touch to the satin ribbon roses. Combining these elements is surprisingly easy and the method is quite simple to master.

The use of fabric shapes eliminates the need for highly elaborate, time-consuming embroidery stitches. The projects are easy to make and suited to our hectic schedules where the desire exists for a creative hobby, though leisure time is so limited.

I also explain the quilting technique that is often used with these designs. Most of the stitches are made through several layers of fabric, preventing the work from puckering and pulling out of shape – something that often happens when you are embroidering on a single layer of fabric. The technique differs from traditional ribbon embroidery, but it is really easy, and the finished project looks so much better than a flat piece of embroidery.

This book combines silk and satin ribbon embroidery with candlewicking and quilting. Silk ribbon is sold by the metre (yard), is soft and pliable and used as an emboidery thread. Only silk ribbon measuring 3–3.5 mm (⅛ in) in width is used, as wider ribbon is not delicate enough for these designs. Satin ribbon, also sold by the metre (yard), is the thicker, more rigid kind of ribbon that has been in use for many years. I use satin ribbon measuring 6–8 mm (¼–⅜ in) to make the satin ribbon roses. This ribbon is far too thick and cumbersome to use for embroidering.

The designs included in this book may seem intricate, but this is their unique appeal. The intricacy of the designs themselves means that you will not need to use involved stitches or complicated techniques to add interest. As I firmly believe that it is the design, and not perfectly formed elaborate embroidery stitches, that determines the end result, the designs are especially suited to beginners attempting this art form. The finished project may appear very detailed, but only the most basic stitches will have been used. More experienced needleworkers will enjoy the fresh, new designs, using stitches of their choice. By combining these designs with a variety of colours, textures, ribbon, threads and beading, you will achieve amazing results. I am certain that many of your creations will become much talked-about family treasures!

HOW DOES THIS BOOK WORK?

Each design is drawn to scale. No enlarging is necessary. The designs are named for easy reference, and appear at the back of the book (pages 65–94).

The first six designs are suitable for framing individually, or for making cushions or quilt squares. Some designs will be joined after tracing each half of the design, as indicated.

The next 16 designs are quarter or half designs. These are joined to form larger designs measuring 30–41 cm (12–16 in) square, and are particularly suitable for making cushions or quilt squares. In this section, there are nine designs measuring 41 cm x 41 cm (16 in x 16 in), which are most suitable for the cushions and quilts. There are six designs measuring 30 cm x 30 cm (12 in x 12 in), suitable for making smaller cushions or quilts. The smaller designs may also be used for making larger quilts, but of course you will need to make more squares to compensate for individual squares being smaller. I would recommend using the first nine designs in this section, each measuring 41 cm x 41 cm (16 in x 16 in), to save time when making quilts. I have also included a design called *Filigree* for those wishing to make a round cushion. Refer to *How do I trace and join the quarter or half designs?* on page 8 for detailed instructions.

The last seven designs are suitable for use on smaller projects like tray-cloths, and also include a design for decorating a beautiful little girl's dress for a wedding or other special occasion.

Most of the designs which I have included can be used for other crafts such as shadow appliqué and quilting, candlewicking and quilting, stencilling, painting on fabric, glued appliqué, trapunto or plain quilting. I have given a brief explanation under *Adapting these designs for other crafts* on page 41. The versatility of the designs makes them an asset to any pattern collector.

HOW DO I TRACE AND JOIN THE QUARTER AND HALF DESIGNS?

The quarter and half designs in this book are all drawn to scale, so no enlarging is necessary.

1. Trace each section of the quarter or half design onto an A4 sheet of good quality tracing paper.

2. Always use a dark or black fineliner pen to do the tracing.

NOTE

Do not trace any symbols indicating colours or stitches onto the tracing paper. This means that the design is uncomplicated and clear, and therefore easier to trace onto the fabric. Once the design has been traced, you will need to refer to the book again for guidance on colours and embroidery stitches. Always remember, however, to number the shapes on the tracing paper.

3. Trace the design as neatly and as accurately as possible. Use a ruler to draw straight lines. The *Monarch* design is an example where straight lines are used. When tracing a circle, for the *Rapture* design for example, use a dotted or broken line. This will allow you to draw a near perfect circle.

4. Make photocopies according to the instructions for each design. Refer to figures 1a and 1b to see how to construct the complete design for *Odyssey* from the four quarter designs.

THE FOUR QUARTERS OF THE ODYSSEY DESIGN ARE TRACED, PHOTOCOPIED AND JOINED

❖ To ensure that the four quarters of the design join accurately, use a photocopier to make copies of the tracing.

❖ To make a normal copy, place the tracing right side down on the copier.

❖ When instructed to make a reversed copy, place the tracing right side up on the photocopier. The black ink will show through the tracing paper when the design is reversed.

❖ Once you have copied all four quarters, use transparent tape to join them carefully. Cut away any excess paper.

One quarter

FIG. 1 TRACE FOUR QUARTERS OF ODYSSEY DESIGN AND JOIN WITH TAPE

NOTE

The first six designs (e.g. Harmony etc.) also need to be traced following step 1. Tracing is necessary, as the symbols and labels indicating stitches and colours should not appear on the tracing paper. This will help to keep the design very 'clean' and uncluttered, thereby making tracing onto fabric much easier. If you make a photocopy from the book, for instance, it is easy to trace a 'g' for 'green' onto the fabric by mistake, and this can be confusing. Always remember to number the shapes, though.

normal copy   reversed copy

tracing right side down on copier   tracing right side up on copier

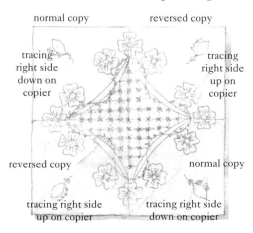

reversed copy   normal copy

tracing right side up on copier   tracing right side down on copier

FIG. 2A RAPTURE DESIGN – *two halves*

FIG. 2B JOIN WITH TAPE

5. To enlarge the quarter or half designs for a wall quilt or Continental pillowcase, for example, make a tracing as described in step 3, and enlarge it on a photocopier. Reverse the tracing as instructed, or copy normally and join the sections using transparent tape.

6. The seven smallest designs can also be enlarged, if desired. Simply copy or enlarge them on a photocopier, working directly from the book.

HINTS

❖ *The neater the initial tracing from the book, the neater the finished article will be. Any lines drawn crooked will remain crooked on your finished square.*

❖ *Use good quality tracing paper that does not crease easily and is transparent.*

❖ *Name each design for reference.*

❖ *When joining designs for circular shapes, concentrate on joining them to form a perfect circle. If flower and leaf shapes are not exact, it will not be noticeable in the design.*

❖ *If you do not have access to a photocopier, trace the design from the book onto tracing paper. Reverse one or two tracings as instructed, and join them carefully.*

MATERIAL REQUIREMENTS

Which fabrics and colours do I choose?

Today we have a wonderful range of fabrics in beautiful colours and textures available to us. Why not make use of these attractive options to embroider a more sophisticated article which is elegant, yet practical? I use polyester silk (polysilk) and taffettas as a background fabric for many of my designs. Polysilk looks like silk (without the cost), it does not crease badly and washes well by hand. Fabric consisting of 100% silk is a beautiful but expensive option. Silky fabrics may not appeal to everybody (the traditionalists might prefer 100% cotton), but I find that, despite their delicate appearance, silky fabrics are far more practical. Cotton may seem more functional, but it creases quite badly once washed. Remember that a quilted article can never be ironed, as this flattens the batting/wadding. Polysilk, on the other hand, does not crease when cleaned according to the instructions on page 14. An added advantage of using silky fabrics is their wide range of beautiful colours.

Silky fabrics quilt better too, as polysilk is more flexible than cotton fabrics, which can be rather unyielding. The beautiful puffiness of hand quilting is lost on cotton fabrics.

Satin fabrics are not suitable for these projects. They do not wash or wear well, and fray badly. The shine of the fabric may also create a rather garish effect. You may like to choose from other fabric types, for example a good quality chintz (glazed cotton) or traditional unbleached calico. Always remember to preshrink cotton fabrics or calico before using them, unlike polysilk, which need not be preshrunk.

HINT

Do not attempt to wash 100% silk fabrics – send them to a reputable dry-cleaner when they become soiled.

Which colours do I use for fabric backgrounds?

The best colour to choose for background fabric for many of these projects is cream. The creamy colour is transparent enough for the design to show through the fabric for tracing. Bearing in mind that most of the projects in this book are likely to become heirlooms which are passed from one generation to the next, a neutral colour like cream is a good choice, as it easily fits in with most colour schemes. You may also like to consider choosing a pale oyster pink, peach or pale green as a background colour for some variation.

Which colours and textures do I use for fabric shapes?

Choose a colour that contrasts with the background, so that the flowers and roses will show up against it. I recommend using a dusty pink, rose pink or peach colour – something resembling the natural colour of the flowers. A navy rose may look rather odd.

Use plain, unpatterned fabric for the roses, so that the embroidery shows up nicely. I generally avoid too many floral or patterned fabrics as the details of the design are lost.

Use green or blue fabric for the leaf shapes. These two colours set off the flowers well, and 'lift' the design at the same time. The fabric chosen for the leaf shapes can be marbled, watermarked or even finely patterned.

A highly effective fabric combination for flowers and leaves can be created by using a silky fabric for the roses or flower shapes, and a glazed cotton or chintz for the leaves. For designs like *Filigree*, use different shades of the same colour, or even a contrasting colour for the flowers. The six designs for the *Baby's quilt* use only one shade of pink or peach fabric for the flower shapes.

Refer to the chapter called *Design Details* (page 43) for details of colours to use for each design. The smaller projects are discussed in the chapter called *Other Projects* (page 59).

HINT
I recommend avoiding dark shades if you are planning an heirloom. If you like primary colours, choose rather dusky shades (like those used in Persian rugs).

How much fabric do I buy?
❖ Make a rough estimate based on fitting in four squares per 1.25 m (1¼ yds) of background fabric, for larger designs for a cushion cover or quilt *(fig. 3).*
❖ To make a cushion you will need a square measuring 57 cm x 57 cm (22½ in x 22½ in) for the front, and a strip of fabric measuring 115 cm x 60 cm (45 in x 24 in) for the two backing pieces. This means that you will need approximately 1.25 m (1¼ yds) of fabric in total per cushion *(fig. 4).*

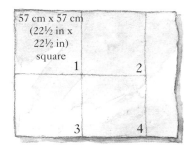

FIG. 3 1.25 M (1¼ YDS)
= 4 SQUARES

❖ For the first six designs in the book – for framing or making cushions – you will need 1 m (1 yd) of background fabric to make four squares. Each square is cut to measure 50 cm x 50 cm (20 in x 20 in).

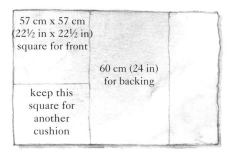

FIG. 4 1.25 M (1¼ YDS) = 1 CUSHION

❖ To determine the fabric requirements for the smaller designs in the book, or the *Baby's quilt*, refer to the chapter called *Other Projects* (page 59).
❖ For a larger quilt, first work out how many squares of background fabric you will need (*see Calculating the number of squares to make up a quilt*, page 37). Divide the total number of squares by 2 (you should be able to fit two squares on the width of the fabric) and multiply the answer by 57 cm (22½ in). If you calculate that you need 12 squares to make a quilt for a double bed, divide this by 2 (12 ÷ 2 = 6), and multiply the answer by 57 cm (22½ in) = 6 x 57 cm (6 x 22½ in) = 3.42 m (3¾ yds).
❖ Refer to the chapter of *Step-by-step instructions* on page 27 to determine the exact measurements for background squares for specific projects.

Which threads and colours
do I use?
Coloured embroidery thread and silk ribbon add depth and look much more interesting than the cream-on-cream look we have become used to. Two different threads are used: the six-strand embroidery skeins (8 m or

8¾ yds) and the silk ribbon thread. These two very different threads enhance the three-dimensional effect which makes ribbon embroidery so interesting. I use silk ribbon that is 3.5 mm (⅛ in) wide, as wider ribbon tends to dominate the design. Ribbon that is 2 mm (⅛ in) wide is too narrow to be effective in these designs. Use embroidery thread instead – it is also more economical. Refer to the chapter on *Design Details* (page 43) for materials and colours to select, and the chapter called *Other Projects* (page 59). Use silk ribbon that is one shade lighter than or the same shade as the darkest pink, peach, green or blue thread.

When making up the designs, the following are important guidelines for choosing colours (whether embroidering the design or combining fabric shapes with embroidery) *(fig. 5)*:
❖ Use slightly darker pink or peachy tones for the larger, main flowers in the design. Remember that these flowers will be the most prominent part of the design, and have the darkest colour. The smaller flowers and leaves will be one or two shades lighter in colour than the main flowers, or may even have a contrasting colour.
❖ Use a medium or light shade of green or blue for all the leaves. Do not, however, use too dark a shade of green or blue, as the leaves will then overshadow the main flowers.
❖ Use the same colour thread as the background square for the quilted squares in the centre of the design (indicated by a broken line), or use a pale shade of pink or peach to complement the colour of the main flowers.
❖ Use a medium shade of pink or peach for any outline of the design, for example circles or straight lines. Too dark a shade will result in the main flowers 'disappearing'.

❖ When using fabric shapes in a design that will not be framed, anchor the raw edges of the fabric shapes and leaves that are glued onto the background with a quilting or running stitch through all the layers, then use a chain stitch or a couched thread (page 20) over the quilting or running stitches so that the raw edges cannot fray when washed. When making a design which is to be framed, it is not necessary to cover the quilting or running stitches with any other stitches, as these items are never washed. The thread used to quilt the raw edges of the shapes should be the same colour as the fabric shapes. Always use embroidery thread – silk ribbon is far too thick.

HINTS

❖ *Remember to use only one, two or three strands of thread for most of the stitches, so that the stitches are not too cumbersome for the design. If you prefer, however, traditional no. 5 or no. 8 cotton thread can be used, although it is probably too thick for intricate designs. Stitches are sewn through all the layers of the work, i.e. fabric, batting/wadding and muslin. For couching, use two to six strands. Refer to the* Stitch codes and legends *(pages 20 and 21) and the individual designs for a guide to which colour and how many strands of thread to use for each stitch.*
❖ *Test coloured thread for colourfastness by washing it in hot water before using it.*

Why use beads?

Beads, if used correctly, can really enhance a design and they can also add a bit of fun to your work! In the same way, a design can soon look gaudy if too many beads are added. Used discreetly, beads provide an almost hidden element, as they are often not noticed at first. Use beads to form the centre of flowers or at each crossover of any quilted squares in a design such as *Odyssey*. Quilted squares are indicated by the dotted (broken) lines found mostly in the centre of designs. Some designs (e.g. *Harmony*) have no quilted squares.

Refer to *Attaching a bead* (page 20) for instructions on how to attach a bead. The positions of round beads are indicated on each design by a ● or a ○. If you are using teardrop-shaped beads, include them in places in the design where indicated by a ◗ shape, instead of a detached chain (page 18). Some designs include beads next to the flower shapes (e.g. *Bordeaux*). The beads then form smaller 'petals' around the flower shapes. Use beads which tone in with the general colour scheme of the design, usually one shade lighter than the main flowers, or use mother-of-pearl, cream, or light green or blue.

Each X indicates the position of a ribbon rose.

Use a medium or light shade of pink or peach for smaller flowers/petals. Use a French or colonial knot to make up this flower.

place green leaves here

place flower badges here

Anchor the fabric shapes to the background using thread to match the colour of the shape. Use a quilting stitch to anchor the shapes.

Use a medium shade of pink or peach for the outline of a design.

Use slightly darker pink or peach tones for the main flowers. Fabric has been used to make up this rose.

Use beads or French/colonial knots in the centre of the flower shapes.

Use a medium shade of green or blue for all the leaves. The stems of flowers/leaves will also be green.

place green leaves here

Use a medium shade of green or blue for leaf shapes.

pink bow

Use a medium shade of pink or peach for the outline.

FIG. 5 THE HARMONY DESIGN: A GUIDE TO COLOURS

Suitable beads to buy are glass seed beads, but I also use the plastic beads found in bridal shops. This gives you a good colour selection.

HINT
Do not use large beads, as they may simply look cumbersome and spoil the design. A larger bead is only suitable to form the centre of a silk ribbon daisy.

Which satin ribbon do I use?
Some designs use roses made from satin ribbon (e.g. *Monarch, Camrose* etc.). The position of each rose is indicated on the design by an X. Use ribbon that is 6–8 mm (¼–⅜ in) wide for all the designs.

If you use ribbon that is too wide, the result is a rose which is out of proportion with the rest of the design and far too dominant. Satin ribbon has a smooth satin side, and a rougher wrong side. These two different sides add texture and charm when the ribbon roses are folded. I usually use a length of ribbon measuring 12 cm (4 ¾ in) to make one rose.

Refer to the section on *How to make satin ribbon roses* (page 22) for detailed instructions on the method to use.

Which batting/wadding do I use?
Batting/wadding is available in various thicknesses. For squares to be used for cushions or quilts, the thicker polyester batting/wadding is used. The 135 g (4 oz) per square or 150 g (5 oz) is ideal. If you are unsure of the weight, judge by the thickness, which should be about 2.5 cm (1 in). The batting/wadding should be soft but not too fluffy, otherwise the 'hairs' are pulled off too easily.

For framed projects (e.g. *Harmony*), choose the very thinnest batting/wadding you can find. I generally use 100 g (3½ oz) or the thinner 67 g (2 oz) batting/wadding (used for quilted jackets) for each square. Thicker batting/wadding is bulky and does not frame well, unless the frame is quite deep and box-like.

HINT
The required batting/wadding is sold per metre (yard) and is not to be confused with polyester stuffing or filling used to fill cushions or soft toys.

Why use muslin for backing the batting/wadding?
Muslin (100% cotton) is used behind the batting/wadding as it prevents the batting/wadding 'hairs' from coming through onto the fabric side of the square as you embroider or quilt. The muslin also gives the article body, thus preventing the finished product from puckering too much. Remember to wash the muslin before using it, and to cut it to exactly the same size as the square of batting/wadding.

HINT
It is not necessary to use muslin on the back of the batting/wadding when making pictures for framing, as the 'hairs' will not pull through as badly to the fabric side of the square. (Cut off any excess 'hairs' using sharp embroidery scissors.) It is also easier to stretch the work for framing if there are only two layers of fabric.

Which fabric is best for backing cushions and quilts?
Cushion covers can look highly professional if the same fabric is used for both front and back, but this really is a matter of individual choice. It may be important to bear in mind, however, that using a silky fabric as a backing

CAMROSE HAS BEEN USED IN EACH CASE, BUT WITH DIFFERENT COLOURS AND FABRICS

may cause the cushion to slip off the chair or sofa more easily. Choose fabrics which are practical and wash well.

For quilts made of silky fabrics or cotton, I suggest that you use a good quality polyester or cotton sheet as a backing. Buy a sheet one size bigger than the quilt (e.g. a king-sized sheet for a double-bed quilt) so that there will be no joins in the fabric. I usually recommend choosing a sheet which is the same colour as the quilt.

I only attach the sheet once the quilt has been joined and made up, as this sheet covers all the embroidery on the reverse (muslin) side of the squares. (This means that you do not have to be too fussy about what the work looks like on the reverse side of the square!) If you find the sheet ballooning too much for your liking, use embroidery thread or silk ribbon to tie off the knots after catching each square at the corner through the sheeting onto the muslin and batting/wadding of the quilt *(fig. 6).*

Which needles and pins do I use?

❖ It is important to use the correct needle. It is frustrating to thread a needle with a small eye, it damages the embroidery thread, as well as removing its sheen. Use a no. 9 crewel embroidery needle for six-strand thread. If you like, use a no. 9 quilting 'between' needle for the quilting stitches, but this is not essential – an embroidery needle will do.

❖ Use a no. 22 chenille needle for sewing with silk ribbon and the traditional no. 5 and no. 8 cottons. When working with silk ribbon, it is important to use a needle with a large eye. The ribbon must always be flat when threaded through the eye (a folded ribbon will result in an untidy stitch).

❖ Always use a sharp needle – a blunt needle will cause snags in silky fabrics.

❖ Use long, sharp steel pins with coloured heads so that no unwelcome guests are left behind. Pins easily disappear into the batting/wadding during completion of the article.

Which quilting hoop do I use and why?

A quilting hoop is essential for this kind of ribbon embroidery. The hoop allows for even tension throughout the quilted article and results in a perfectly smooth finish. I always use as large a hoop as the design allows, so that I am able to embroider all or most of the stitches without having to move the hoop and thereby change the tension. There is no need to tack the layers of fabric together when using a hoop, as they are unable to move once pulled taut in the frame.

There is a significant difference between an embroidery hoop and a quilting hoop. A quilting hoop is thicker in order to hold all the layers together. The wood is about 2 cm (just less than an inch) thick and is tightened with a wing nut, not a screw.

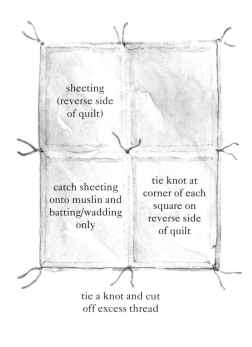

sheeting (reverse side of quilt)

catch sheeting onto muslin and batting/wadding only

tie knot at corner of each square on reverse side of quilt

tie a knot and cut off excess thread

FIG. 6 TO ATTACH BACKING TO QUILT

An embroidery hoop is much thinner, as it only needs to hold one layer of fabric. This kind of hoop is tightened by a round screw.

❖ A quilting hoop with a diameter of 46 cm (18 in) is used when making the cushion and larger quilt squares or squares for the wall quilt (*see* page 59).

❖ A quilting hoop with a diameter of 35.5 cm (14 in) is used when making designs such as *Harmony* or *Bordeaux.*

❖ A quilting hoop with a diameter of 41 cm (16 in) is used when making the *Six-block baby's quilt (see* page 60).

HINTS

❖ *If you find that the design is too small for the hoop you have, cut the background square 5 cm (2 in) larger all round than the size of your hoop. Do the same with the batting/wadding and muslin. Draw the design and outline of the pattern onto the centre of the fabric square, embroider and cut to size once completed. Don't forget to draw the outline (for example, the outline or shape of the collar or panel of the dress) onto the centre of the square – it is very difficult to draw a neat shape onto the fabric once it has been quilted.*

❖ *Always try to use a hoop large enough to accommodate most of the design or the whole design. Using a hoop which is too small means that you will have to move it to complete the work, making it impossible to achieve a perfectly smooth article. The hoop may also damage the embroidered stitches if it is moved.*

Why use a pencil for tracing onto fabric?

I prefer not to use water-soluble pens for tracing, as the tips of these pens are too thick for these intricate designs. I usually use a medium to soft lead pencil (an HB or B pencil). Lightly drawn onto the fabric, the pencil lines disappear into the folds as you quilt, and are covered by the stitching as you sew. As pencil lines do not fade, wash out or rub out once drawn, it is very important to use a sharp pencil to make thin, fine lines. A 3B pencil is only used when tracing the shapes onto the iron-on Vilene or fusible webbing. Use a ruler to draw straight lines, as a crooked, hand-drawn line cannot be rubbed out.

Which other materials or equipment do I need?

❖ a clean steam iron or an iron with a protective cover to prevent scorching (remember to adjust the temperature)
❖ transparent tape
❖ a ruler measuring approximately 45–50 cm (18–20 in)
❖ a pair of sharp dressmakers' scissors, as well as a pair of small, sharp embroidery scissors
❖ a sewing machine – use an 80 or 90 Universal needle for all projects
❖ a sunny window or a glass table with a light underneath it, for tracing
❖ a 3B pencil, used only for tracing onto iron-on Vilene or fusible webbing
❖ an HB or B pencil for tracing the design onto the fabric
❖ a black fineliner pen for tracing
❖ several A4 sheets of good quality tracing paper
❖ a leather or steel thimble (optional)
❖ polyester filling, if you will be making cushions
❖ a soft glue stick, if you are using fabric shapes (*see* page 31) (liquid glue will mark the fabric)
❖ a T-square to draw squares (optional)
❖ fabric for the frill, binding or cording if you are making a cushion
❖ Vilene for using with the fabric shapes – choose an iron-on Vilene/fusible webbing of medium thickness (check to see that it has a shiny iron-on side before buying it) to back the flower and leaf shapes (*see Make the fabric shapes* on page 28)

❖ fabric for outer borders, if you have chosen to finish a cushion cover with a coloured border (*see* the *Monarch* cushion cover on page 26, far right). You will need a rectangle measuring 57 x 25 cm (23 in x 10 in) in a complementary shade that will enhance the design, much like a frame.

HINTS WHEN EMBROIDERING

1. Use the best quality fabrics you can afford to ensure heirloom quality.
2. To ensure a good finish, trace the design as neatly and precisely as possible, using a ruler to draw straight lines.
3. When making a quilt, draw a square measuring the required size on a cardboard sheet and make a template, so that all the fabric squares will be exactly the same size.
4. Cut the square of background fabric, batting/wadding and muslin at least 5–8 cm (2–3 in) larger than the hoop. Draw the required square size and design onto the centre of the fabric square and cut to the required size only once the work is complete.
5. Keep the layers of batting/wadding and fabric in the hoop taut at all times. Ensure a smooth finish by tightening your work every time you pick it up.
6. Never iron quilted articles – the heat from the iron flattens the batting/wadding and the raised effect created by the quilting disappears.
7. Always iron on the wrong side of the fabric. Select the correct temperature setting before pressing. Use a silk temperature setting for polysilk and taffetta.
18. It takes time and practice to develop fine embroidery skills. Don't be deterred by imperfections – these designs are detailed enough to hide most 'mistakes'. Do not unpick your work unless it is absolutely necessary – the charm of your article may well be lost if it looks too perfect.

A GUIDE TO MATTRESS SIZES

A guide to approximate mattress sizes is given below. Please measure your mattress before beginning a quilt.
TWIN OR SINGLE BED:
92 cm x 190 cm (3 ft x 6 ft 3 in)
THREE-QUARTER BED:
110 cm x 190 cm (3 ft 5 in x 6 ft 3 in)
DOUBLE BED:
150 cm x 190 cm (4 ft 6 in x 6 ft 3 in)
QUEEN-SIZE BED (NOT UK):
153 cm x 190 cm (5 ft x 6 ft 3 in)
KING-SIZE BED:
180 cm x 190 cm (5 ft 10 in x 6 ft 3 in)
EXTRA-LONG KING-SIZE BED:
180 cm x 200 cm (5 ft 10 in x 6 ft 7 in)

WASHING INSTRUCTIONS

Wiping an article

Consider just wiping a soiled article, before deciding to wash it. Polysilks are easily wiped clean and I always clean my cushions, quilts and wall-hangings this way. Wiping instead of washing gives the article a longer life span. It is important, however, to follow these steps carefully to prevent watermarks from forming.
1. Take a clean, damp cloth and a bar of ordinary white soap.
2. Soap the cloth as you would if you were bathing.
3. Wring out the excess soap and water until the cloth is damp, not wet.
4. Carefully wipe the mark on the cushion or quilt square.
5. Do not stop there, but continue to wipe the entire surface so that the whole square is damp. This prevents watermarks from forming.
6. Place the damp article in the sun so that it can dry quickly, again trying to prevent watermarks from forming.
7. PLEASE NOTE: 100% silk fabric cannot be wiped or washed. Use a reputable dry-cleaner only!

HERE THE ODYSSEY DESIGN IS USED FOR TWO DIFFERENT BUT EQUALLY LOVELY SQUARES

2. Remove any cushion inners before washing their covers.

3. Place the article to be washed in a basin or bath of cool or tepid water (*not* hot water) to which mild soap flakes have been added. Always make sure that the soap flakes have dissolved in the water first, otherwise they may leave marks on the fabric.

4. Soak the article for a few minutes, then rub the soiled area gently with your fingertips to remove any marks. If you are washing a quilt, fill the bath with enough water so that the entire quilt can be submerged.

5. Drain the water from the basin or bath.

6. Set the article aside or simply move it to the end of the bath furthest from the taps and refill the basin or bath with cool water. Soak the article for a few minutes again, to remove all soapy residue. Continue soaking and rinsing in this way until the rinsing water is clean and soap-free.

7. Drain the water from the basin or bath again, and gently pat the article dry between two towels, keeping it flat at all times. (Make sure that the towels are colourfast!) Do not be tempted to wring the article dry. If you are washing a quilt, drain the water and, using several towels, pat the quilt gently to remove as much water as possible before lifting the quilt from the bath.

8. It is preferable to dry the washed article in a shady area. Peg cushion covers by two of the corners. Spread a quilt out evenly over two or three strands of a washing line.

9. Choose a hot or windy day so that the article dries quickly, preventing watermarks from forming.

10. If it is absolutely necessary to iron the article, hold a steam iron close to the surface of the fabric, but do not touch it. Allow the steam to iron out the creases. Try, as far as possible, to avoid ironing a quilted article.

HINTS

✤ *If you notice a watermark on the square once the article is dry, repeat steps 1–6.*

✤ *It is not easy to wipe cotton fabrics clean in the way I have just described, as the stains often tend to 'set'. It is best to wash stained cotton fabrics instead (refer to the instructions on the right).*

Washing an article

1. First test all the fabrics you have used in making the article for colour-fastness. Use a few damp, white paper or fabric napkins and gently rub each colour fabric. If any colour is transferred to the napkin, do not wash the article – it is not colourfast.

RIBBON EMBROIDERY

Although this kind of embroidery has been with us for a long time now, it has in recent years become one of the most popular art forms of its kind. Ribbon embroidery is surprisingly easy to master. The chosen stitches require little expertise and will amaze beginners with their simplicity. Two kinds of ribbon are used: silk ribbon, which is used in the same way as ordinary embroidery thread; and satin ribbon, which is used for making the small ribbon roses.

I *begin* the embroidery stitches by making a knot in the thread, rather than with a backstitch – embroidery thread is expensive and making a knot is more economical. The completed article may not be as neat at the back as it would be if you were using a backstitch, but usually nobody sees the back anyway! If you prefer, however, start with a few backstitches.

Silk ribbon work cannot be started with a knot, as the knot will be too large and bulky. Leave a tail of about 2.5 cm (1 in) when starting work with silk ribbon, and catch the tail as you make the second or third stitch.

To *end off* embroidery threads where there are two to six strands, separate the strands to make two threads. Make five to eight knots, one on top of the other. As an alternative, make a few backstitches, or simply run the thread underneath the adjoining stitches to end off.

To end off silk ribbon, catch the tail end of the ribbon when making the next stitch, or backstitch by inserting the needle through the tail end of the ribbon into the backing and batting/wadding to secure it (*see Using silk ribbon* on pages 33–34 for detailed instructions on how to thread a chenille needle with silk ribbon).

Each small satin ribbon rose is made individually (*see How to make satin ribbon roses* on page 22). The roses are attached to the background fabric where required after completion (*see Attaching the roses* on page 24).

STITCH GUIDES

1. Quilting or running stitch

❖ SEWN THROUGH ALL LAYERS

Use two strands of embroidery thread. Push the needle through all the layers of the fabric 'sandwich' *(fig. 1a)*. Use up and down stab stitches (*see Note*, below). The stitches must each be about 2–3 mm ($\frac{1}{16}$–$\frac{1}{8}$ in) long and evenly spaced. *Pull tight* to form a gully

NOTE

Stab stitches simply mean that only 'half' or one stitch is made at a time (fig. 1b).

2. Backstitch

❖ SEWN THROUGH ALL LAYERS

Use two strands of embroidery thread. Backstitch is useful for defining lines of small curves. *Pull tight* as for the quilting stitch *(fig. 2)*.

3. Stem stitch

❖ SEWN THROUGH ALL LAYERS

Use one or two strands of embroidery thread (one strand for very fine detail). As for the quilting or running stitch, bring the needle up from the back of the work along the pencilled line on the fabric. Make a running stitch and pull the thread taut to the back of the work. Re-insert the needle halfway back, pulling the thread taut to the front. This is also a 'stab stitch' (*see Note,* above). Thus, for this type of quilted stem stitch, an ordinary running stitch is made on the fabric (top) side of the work and a backstitch is made

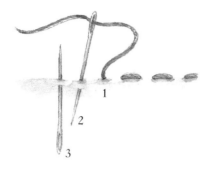

FIG. 1A QUILTING/RUNNING STITCH

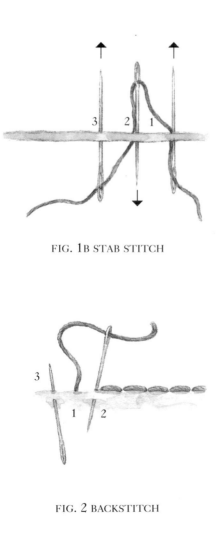

FIG. 1B STAB STITCH

FIG. 2 BACKSTITCH

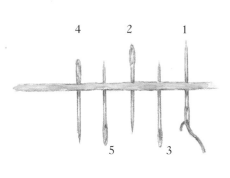

FIG. 3A STEM STITCH

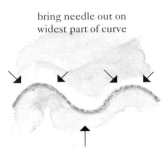

bring needle out on widest part of curve

FIG. 3B STEM STITCH

taut while winding it around the needle for the next knot. This prevents the previous knot from being too loose. For larger dots, use silk ribbon wound around the needle once. You can also use French knots to fill a shape. Make the knots close together to form the shape. You may like to outline the shape with stem stitches first.

on the muslin and batting/wadding (back) side of the work *(fig. 3a)*. Bring the needle up on the widest part of the curve, i.e. on the outside of the curve *(fig. 3b)*. On a straight line, it does not matter on which side of the stitch you bring out the needle and the thread.

4. Chain stitch

❖ SEWN THROUGH ONLY THE TOP LAYER OF THE FABRIC AND PART OF THE BATTING/WADDING

Use two strands of embroidery thread for making a chain. Bring the needle from the back of the work to the front at the starting point of the chain *(fig. 4)*. Make a loop with the thread. The needle then returns to the place where the thread emerged, and the thread loops underneath the needle. Bring the needle out at the opposite curve of the chain and, making sure that the thread is still looped, gently pull the thread to form a chain stitch. Insert the needle back into the previous chain. Do not pull too tight.

5. French knot and French knot filling

❖ SEWN THROUGH ALL LAYERS

Use one or two strands of embroidery thread (one strand for very fine detail). Bring the needle from the back of the fabric to the front *(fig. 5)*. Wind the thread around the needle three times. Push the needle back through the fabric, close to the point where it was brought through the first time.

Pull the thread while the needle is still in the fabric and the batting/wadding, and pull it down onto the fabric until the knot lies snugly on the fabric. At the same time, pull the thread slightly to tighten the knot around the needle.

Hold the thread taut with your free hand. Now pull the needle to the back of the work, pulling gently on the thread at the back of the work until the knot lies neatly on the fabric. Insert the needle from the back to the next dot, pulling the thread to the top of the work. Pull the thread taut and keep it

6. Detached chain

❖ SEWN THROUGH ONLY THE TOP LAYER OF FABRIC AND PART OF THE BATTING/WADDING, BUT THE ANCHORING STITCH IS MADE THROUGH ALL THE LAYERS

When making a detached chain, each stitch is held down separately with the thread you are working with.

Use silk ribbon wherever a larger teardrop shape ◗ is drawn. Use two strands of embroidery thread where a smaller teardrop shape ◖ is drawn. Make a single chain as for the chain stitch *(fig. 4)*, but anchor each shape by inserting the needle to the back of the work 2 mm (1/16 in) away from the rounded part of the chain *(fig. 6)*. Do not pull the thread too tight or the chain will close. A chain made from silk ribbon should look like a petal that has fallen onto the fabric (neither too loose nor too tight).

HINT
To create an interesting variation, make the anchoring stitch a little longer and you will form an attractive, bell-like stitch.

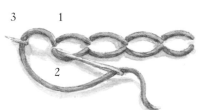

FIG. 4 CHAIN STITCH

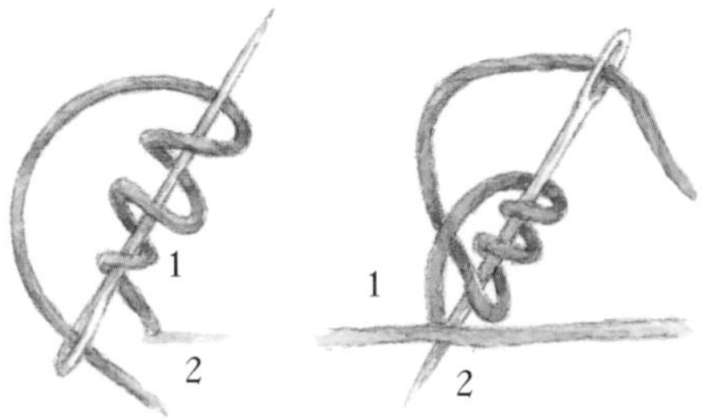

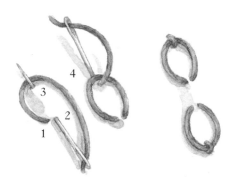

FIG. 5 FRENCH KNOT

FIG. 6 DETACHED CHAIN/LAZY DAISY

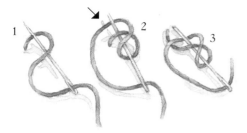

FIG. 7 COLONIAL KNOT

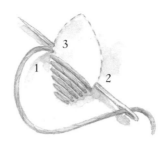

FIG. 8 SATIN STITCH

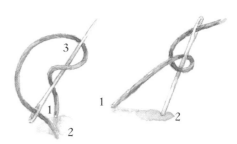

FIG. 9 EXTENDED FRENCH KNOT

7. Lazy daisy

❖ SEWN ONLY THROUGH THE TOP LAYER OF FABRIC AND PART OF THE BATTING/WADDING, BUT THE ANCHORING STITCH IS MADE THROUGH ALL THE LAYERS

Use two strands of embroidery thread or, to form a larger daisy shape, use silk ribbon instead of the thread.

Follow the same procedure as for the detached chain, but form the loops into a flower. Add a bead to the centre so that it looks like a daisy.

8. Colonial knot

❖ SEWN THROUGH ALL LAYERS

A colonial knot is slightly bigger than a French knot and can be used instead of the latter. Use one or two strands of embroidery thread or silk ribbon.

Bring the needle through the back of the fabric to the front, just to the left of the dot indicating where the knot is to be made *(fig. 7)*. Hold the embroidery thread lightly between your thumb and forefinger. Push the needle under the thread from left to right, then twist the thread over and under the point of the needle to form a figure of eight. Insert the needle through the fabric to the right of where the needle first emerged, pulling the needle and thread firmly to the back of the fabric and tightening as for a French knot. Continue in this way, bringing the needle through to the right of the next dot.

9. Satin stitch

❖ SEWN THROUGH ALL LAYERS

Use two strands of embroidery thread. This can be used as an alternative filling stitch, although it can be difficult to keep tidy – rather use a French knot filling. Satin stitch consists of straight, even stitches worked closely together *(fig. 8)*. For a neater result, begin satin stitch at the widest point of the area that is to be covered and work towards the edge. Turn the work around to complete the uncovered part. The stitches must not overlap. Be careful that you do not pull the thread so tightly that the fabric puckers. Finish off by running the needle under a few stitches at the back of the article.

10. Extended French knot

❖ SEWN THROUGH ALL LAYERS

Silk ribbon is ideal for this stitch as it is thick, thus creating very effective 'petals' to form a flower *(fig. 9)*. Follow the same procedure as for a French knot, but instead of inserting the needle back where the thread first came through, insert it 3–4 mm (⅛ in) away from the thread. When using embroidery thread, wind it around the

VICTORIAN TRELLIS IS ONE OF THE DESIGNS USED FOR THE FOUR-BLOCK QUILT

needle three times. When using silk ribbon, wind it around the needle once. Make four, five or six petals to form a daisy. Use embroidery thread to attach a bead in the centre of the daisy.

11. Couching

❖ TWO TO SIX STRANDS OF THREAD LIE LOOSELY ON TOP OF THE FABRIC; ONE TO TWO STRANDS ANCHOR THIS THREAD THROUGH ALL THE LAYERS

Couching is used for outlining or for filling in. Thicker strands of thread are laid on the surface of the fabric and held in place by small, straight couching stitches using thinner thread.

Depending on the detail of the design, use two to six strands of thread and a no. 22 chenille needle for the thicker (laid) thread. Cut the thread 1 m (1 yd) long and thread it through the chenille needle. Make a knot at the long end. To anchor the laid threads, use only one to two strands of a shorter thread, about 40 cm (16 in) long, in the same colour, and an embroidery needle. Make a knot in this shorter thread. Bring the laid

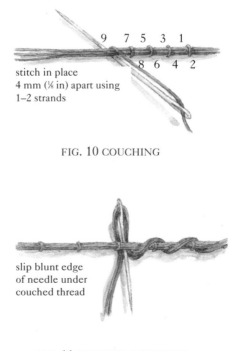

stitch in place
4 mm (⅛ in) apart using
1–2 strands

FIG. 10 COUCHING

slip blunt edge
of needle under
couched thread

FIG. 11 WHIPPED COUCHING

threads from the back of the fabric to the front. Allow the threads to lie loosely on the pencilled line (*fig. 10*).

Bring the shorter couching thread from the back of the fabric to the front, 3 mm (⅛ in) from where the laid thread came through. Stitch or anchor the laid thread in place by inserting the embroidery needle back over and under the laid thread. Space these stitches about 3 mm (⅛ in) apart and sew the laid thread along the pencilled line. Pull the laid thread taut while you sew so that it lies evenly along the pencilled line, with no kinks.

For filling in flower stems, for example, first outline stems with couching as above, then insert the needle from the back and bring up next to the outline, filling up spaces in-between with couching so that there are no gaps between stitches.

12. Whipped or raised couching

❖ SEWN ONLY UNDERNEATH THE COUCHED TWO- TO SIX-STRAND THREADS

After stitching the two- or six-strand threads along the pencilled line, re-thread the chenille needle with two to six strands of matching embroidery thread. Cut the thread 1 m (1 yd) long.

Insert the blunt side of the needle under and over each segment of the couched thread (*fig. 11*). The fabric is not sewn at all.

13. Attaching a bead

❖ SEWN THROUGH ALL LAYERS

Use two strands of embroidery thread. Attach the bead by running the thread once or twice through the eye of the bead, as you would when sewing on a 'one-eyed' button (*fig. 12*).

14. Honeycomb stitch

❖ WOVEN STITCHES LIE LOOSELY ON TOP OF THE FABRIC, ANCHORED AT INTERSECTIONS THROUGH ALL LAYERS

This is another form of couching and is useful in an area that requires heavy shading, e.g. the centre of a flower. It is not suitable for large areas, however – rather use plain couching (*see Couching*). Use two strands of embroidery thread and an embroidery needle (*fig. 13*).

STITCH CODES AND LEGENDS

The stitches to use for each design are indicated by the use of lines:
❖ A solid line denotes that stem stitch, backstitch, couching or honeycomb stitch can be used (any of these).
❖ A broken line indicates quilting stitches or running stitches.
❖ Dots indicate French or colonial knots and beads.
❖ Teardrops indicate a detached chain. A teardrop bead can also be used where small teardrops are indicated.

These are mere guidelines – be as creative as you wish, using stitches of your choice. The colour combinations are also only suggestions, but I would recommend that you do not stray too far from the guidelines I have offered.

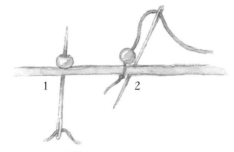

FIG. 12 ATTACHING A BEAD

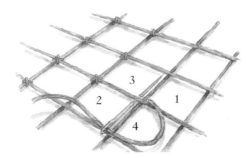

FIG. 13 HONEYCOMB STITCH

STITCH	ALTERNATIVE	PATTERN CODE	COLOUR
QUILTING (use embroidery thread – two strands)	Back stitch Stem stitch Couching Chain stitch	- - - - - - - - - - - - Broken line	For background quilting, e.g. centre blocks in the design, use cream or a complementary shade. Use green or colour of leaves to quilt around the fabric shapes to anchor them to the background.
STEM STITCH (use embroidery thread – two strands)	Chain stitch Back stitch Couching Quilting	～～～～～ Solid line	Use darkest pink or peach to embroider main flower shapes. Use green to embroider leaf shapes and veins. Use medium to dark shades to embroider the outline of the design.
FRENCH KNOTS (use embroidery thread – one or two strands, or silk ribbon)	Colonial knots Beads	o ∴ o o '	Use a slightly darker shade or the shade that matches fabric flowers for their centres (if using beads, use one shade lighter). Use darker shades of pink or peach to embroider the flower if not using fabric shapes. Use silk ribbon to make knots where there is a large o.
EXTENDED FRENCH KNOT (use silk ribbon or embroidery thread – one or two strands)	Lazy daisy	✳ ✳ ✳	Use as indicated on the design.
COUCHING (use embroidery thread – two to six strands)	Quilting Back stitch Satin stitch	～～～～～ Solid line	Use as indicated on the design.
HONEYCOMB STITCH (use embroidery thread – two strands)	Back stitch Stem stitch Quilting	▨▨▨▨ Usually found in centre of flowers	Use as indicated on the design.
CHAIN STITCH (use embroidery thread – two strands)	French knots sewn close together Couching Stem stitch Quilting	A solid line or ⌇⌇⌇⌇ chain	Use as indicated on the design.
DETACHED CHAIN AND LAZY DAISY (use embroidery thread – two strands, or silk ribbon)	Extended French knot Teardrop bead	⬖ For small teardrops use two strands embroidery thread. ⬖ For larger teardrops for leaves use silk ribbon ✳ ✳ ✳ Lazy daisy – use embroidery cotton or silk ribbon	Use as indicated on the design. Use as indicated on the design. Use as indicated on the design.
FRENCH KNOT FILLING (use embroidery thread – two strands)	Satin stitch Couching	❀ Smaller buds or circles ✿ To make rose or flower shapes	Use as indicated on the design.

HOW TO MAKE SATIN RIBBON ROSES

Each satin ribbon rose is made separately and then attached to the background fabric. This kind of rose is easy to make and the step-by-step instructions which follow have been written especially for the beginner. There are several methods to use when making up the rose, but I find the one offered here the easiest and quickest. Ribbon roses should not be the most dominant feature of the design, as they can seem rather gaudy. Used in the correct proportion, however, the roses add a most interesting dimension to the design. I usually use satin ribbon that is 6 mm (¼ in) or 8 mm (⅜ in) wide and 12 cm (4¾ in) in length (*see Which satin ribbon do I use?* on page 12 for more information). Roses made with wider ribbon are useful for adorning items such as shoes, hat boxes, hair-clips and small baskets. The roses are glued onto these items. Similar wide satin ribbon roses can form a beautiful feature on a wedding dress or other item of clothing for a special occasion.

Satin ribbon roses are not used for all the projects. They are not practical for a baby's quilt, for instance, as they may be worked loose and swallowed. Silk ribbon is ideal for a baby's quilt using flat stitches and quilting.

NOTE
Adding satin ribbon roses is an optional step in making these designs. If you would rather not use ribbon roses, use silk ribbon or embroidery thread to make detached chains, lazy daisies or a few French or colonial knots to cover each X on the design.

Step-by-step instructions
1. Thread an embroidery needle with two strands of embroidery thread or machine thread in the same colour as the satin ribbon. Make a knot at the long end of the thread.

2. Cut a length of ribbon measuring approximately 12 cm (4¾ in).

3. Hold the ribbon horizontally so that the wrong (dull) side is facing you.

4. Begin folding at the end of the ribbon that is on your right. Fold over about 6 mm (¼ in) of the ribbon to the wrong side *(fig. 1)*.

5. Fold the folded section of ribbon in half, so that the fold is about 3 mm (⅛ in) wide *(fig. 2)*.

6. Start rolling the folded ribbon from right to left, making three or four rolls *(fig. 3)*. You are now forming the centre of the rose. Do not allow these initial rolls to be too loose, or the finished rose will not have a neat, well-formed shape.

HINT
It may be easier to use your fingernails (rather than your fingertips) to hold the ribbon when rolling it up.

7. Use the needle and thread to sew the little roll in place at the base, using a whipstitch (or any stitch you like) *(fig. 4)*. Pinch the top of the roll between your fingernails to hold it together whilst sewing.

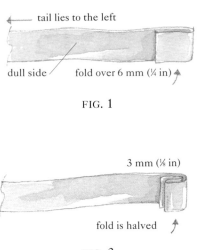

tail lies to the left

dull side   fold over 6 mm (¼ in)

FIG. 1

3 mm (⅛ in)

fold is halved

FIG. 2

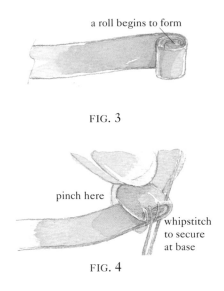

a roll begins to form

FIG. 3

pinch here

whipstitch to secure at base

FIG. 4

NOTE
Make sure that the long tail of the ribbon is still lying horizontally, with the tail on the left of the roll. If you turn the roll so that the ribbon tail lies to the right, you will sew up the top part of the roll by mistake and be unable to continue.

Do not be too concerned about the neatness of your stitches. They won't be seen at all once the rose has been completed.

8. Leave the needle and thread hanging at this stage, and fold the tail of the ribbon over towards you (forwards), at an angle of 45° *(fig. 5)*. The satin side of the ribbon should be facing you and the tail should be hanging vertically. Hold the roll in your right hand, gripping it with your fingernails, and fold further with the left hand.

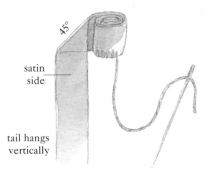

45°

satin side

tail hangs vertically

FIG. 5

9. Hold the tail with your left hand (fingernails) at the *folded* part of the ribbon and pull the left hand *upwards*, lifting this fold as the right hand rolls the fold around the stitched roll *(figs. 6a, 6b and 6c)*. The tail, which was hanging vertically, should now have been pulled back to the horizontal position.

NOTE

The fold must be lifted as you roll, as this ensures that the centre of the flower and the outer petals are level (fig. 6b). When the centre of the flower protrudes too much, the flower is unattractive.

10. Lift with the left hand, and roll with the right hand, until the fold has disappeared around the central roll (i.e. all rolled up). The tail of the ribbon is lying horizontally once again and the satin side is facing you.

NOTE

Stop rolling once the fold has been rolled up. If you were to roll beyond the fold, the rose would 'close up' and look odd.

11. Hold the roll at the top, pinching it between the nails of your left hand. Sew the roll together as before, but insert the needle higher up (halfway up) so that the lifted rolls will be stitched together *(fig. 7)*.

NOTE

To avoid any confusion, ensure that the tail of the ribbon always lies to the left, even when you are stitching the roll together.

12. Summary of the method:
❖ ROLL: Make a few rolls to form the centre of the rose.
❖ STITCH: Stitch the roll together neatly at the base.
❖ FOLD: Make a 45° fold, so that satin side of the ribbon faces you and the tail hangs vertically.

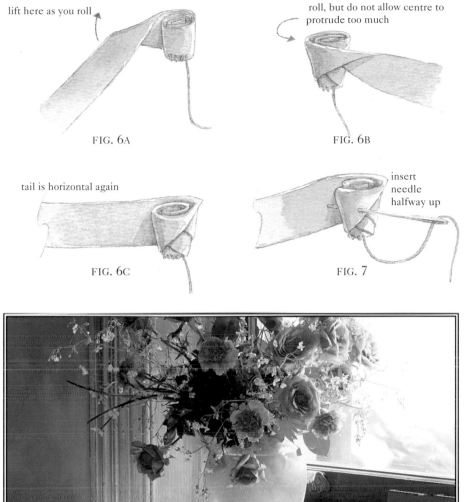

lift here as you roll

FIG. 6A

roll, but do not allow centre to protrude too much

FIG. 6B

tail is horizontal again

FIG. 6C

insert needle halfway up

FIG. 7

RIBBON ROSES DECORATE THE OUTLINE OF THE ROSE CHAIN DESIGN ON THIS CUSHION

❖ ROLL: Roll (lifting the fold) until the fold has been 'all rolled up'.

❖ STITCH: Sew the layers forming the roll together again.

❖ FOLD: Fold towards you at 45° again (*see* step 13).

Remember to repeat the above sequence (roll, stitch, fold; roll, stitch, fold), and it will be quite easy.

13. Fold the tail of the ribbon towards you again, at an angle of 45° (*see* step 8). This time the wrong (dull) side of the ribbon will be facing you (*fig. 8*). The dull side adds texture to the rose and I find this attractive. The ribbon tail will be hanging vertically again.

14. Hold the top of the fold in the left hand (using your fingernails) and lift as before, while the right hand rolls the fold until it 'disappears'. Pinch the top of the rose with the left hand and stitch to secure. Do not stitch at the base this time, but closer to the centre of the rose (i.e. higher up), as you did in step 11.

N O T E

If you find that your rose is becoming flat, you are pulling the stitches too tight.

15. Fold the ribbon tail forward at an angle of 45° again, roll and stitch in place as before.

16. At this stage the rose may already be the desired size. If not, fold, roll and stitch as before, until you have reached a size that you like.

17. TO END OFF Fold the tail of the ribbon over towards you again, at an angle of 45°. The tail should hang vertically. Now roll up half of the fold, and with the ribbon tail still hanging vertically, pinch the top of the rose together and stitch the tail to the base of the rose (*fig. 9*). Cut off the excess ribbon tail close to the stitching, *but leave the needle and thread attached.* This thread will be used to attach the rose to the background fabric.

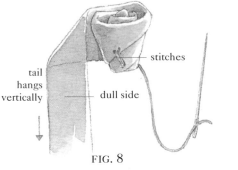

FIG. 8

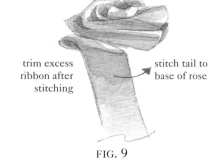

FIG. 9

N O T E

The bottom part of the rose (i.e. the base) will not be seen. This is the part that will be stitched down onto the background fabric or glued onto the ballet shoes. Any loose ends that are showing can be tucked in as you attach the rose, or glue it on. It is not necessary to singe the raw ends of the ribbon – too many of my students have burnt their fingers in the process!

H I N T

If you prefer making the roses with only the satin side showing, fold the tail forwards, then backwards again after stitching to secure the roll each time. Use angles of 45° when folding, as before.

Attaching the roses

If you look at the designs included in this book, you will notice that the satin ribbon roses are not indicated as rose shapes. I have simply indicated the *position* of each rose by using an X on the design. If you draw rose shapes on the fabric, there is a chance that the pencil marks will not be covered completely once the roses have been attached.

The ribbon roses are sewn on by inserting the needle and attached thread from the top layer of fabric to the back, and re-inserting from the back to the front through one of the rose 'petals'. In this way a rose that does not meet your expectations in terms of shape can be neatened and reshaped as you sew. I therefore suggest that you give every rose you have made a chance, without being too fussy about its initial shape!

1. Place the ribbon rose on top of an X on the design and insert the needle through the fabric, pulling the thread to the back so that rose lies snugly against the background.

2. Bring the needle up from the back, in-between two petals of the rose. Pull the thread taut and make sure that the rose has not moved away from the fabric.

3. Insert the needle from the top again, about 2 mm (1⁄16 in) away from where the thread came out, in-between the same petal folds. Pull taut from the back.

4. Repeat this procedure, sewing in-between several of the petal folds until the rose is attached securely.

5. Tuck in any stray petals or ends as you sew. The rose can be opened up more by catching the outer petals and sewing them down onto the fabric.

6. If the centre of the rose protrudes too much, bring the needle up from the back of the work through the centre of the rose. Catch one of the rolls in the centre of the rose, then take the needle to the back again, pulling the thread tight, thereby pulling the centre of the rose inwards.

7. Tie off all loose threads, making several knots on top of one another.

N O T E

If your thread has become too short, tie it off at the back and use a fresh thread knotted at the long end.

HOW TO MAKE PUFFED THREE-DIMENSIONAL SHAPES

The fabric roses in some of the designs (e.g. *Harmony*) have been made to look three-dimensional. This technique is included here for more experienced appliqué artists and does not form an important feature of the designs. The brief instructions on this page offer a guide to making the puffed shapes.

What do I need?

Begin by referring to the section called *What do I need?* (page 27) in the chapter titled *Step-by-Step Instructions*. You will also need the following:

❖ 10 cm x 10 cm (4 in x 4 in) of thin batting/wadding for each puffed rose
❖ 10 cm x 10 cm (4 in x 4 in) of fabric in the same colour as the fabric rose
❖ a sewing machine that has been set on a fine zigzag stitch or satin stitch
❖ machine thread in the same colour as the fabric rose
❖ ordinary brown paper to back each rose shape during appliqué

THE SOLITAIRE DESIGN HERE USES PUFFED, THREE-DIMENSIONAL SHAPES IN THE CENTRE

Step-by-step instructions

1. Follow the step-by-step instructions on pages 27–30 (end with step 6, *Pin the design to the background fabric square*).
2. Before gluing all the fabric shapes onto the background fabric, decide which roses you would like to make into three-dimensional shapes. In the *Harmony* design, for instance, the roses labelled *A* and *B* would be ideal.
3. Glue each cut out rose shape onto a square of batting/wadding *(fig. 1)*.
4. Place the batting/wadding, flower shape facing up, on the wrong side of the backing fabric square *(fig. 1)*.
5. Complete the layered fabric 'sandwich' by pinning the batting/wadding and fabric squares onto the brown paper, keeping the fabric rose shape facing upwards *(fig. 1)*.

6. Zigzag or use satin stitches around the raw edge of the rose shape all round, stitching through all the layers.
7. Tear off the brown paper backing and trim away the excess fabric layers right next to the zigzagged edge using small, sharp embroidery scissors.

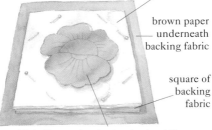

square of batting/wadding

brown paper underneath backing fabric

square of backing fabric

fabric flower glued to batting/wadding

FIG 1. PIN ALL LAYERS TOGETHER

8. Now proceed with step 7, *Glue and position the fabric shapes* (page 00), but apply glue only to the centre of each puffed rose shape. Firmly press down the centre of each puffed shape, leaving the zigzagged edge free.
9. Stitch the puffed shapes down first, as you have used very little glue. Do not anchor these shapes around the edges, but use backstitches or stem stitches along the pencilled lines. Pull the stitches tight, flattening the batting/wadding along the stitch lines. The shapes will lift along the loose edges.
10. When embroidering the design, ignore *Start embroidery* (page 34) and proceed with *Embroidering the detail on the fabric flower and leaf shapes* (page 35).

STEP-BY-STEP INSTRUCTIONS

The basic steps that have been set out here will guide even the most inexperienced needleworker through the various stages of ribbon embroidery. Some of the designs in the book use both the silk ribbon embroidery and satin ribbon rose detail; other designs have no satin ribbon roses at all and use only silk and cotton thread.

The designs combine fabric flowers and leaves, drawn and cut out on iron-on Vilene/fusible webbing. These shapes are then glued onto the background square and sewn on with a quilting or chain stitch or couching. The shapes are really easy to make, even for inexperienced needleworkers, and save the huge amount of time and effort that would usually be spent filling shapes with embroidery stitches.

The appliquéd fabric shapes add colour and texture to the designs and combine well with ribbon embroidery, balancing and enhancing the embroidery work at the same time.

I do encourage you to try this unique method of embroidery!

NOTE
If you decide not to use fabric shapes at all, ignore the iron-on Vilene, and the roses and leaf shapes in the chapter called Design Details *(pages 43–570) and buy extra skeins of embroidery thread instead.*

If you have chosen to embroider all the shapes in the design (*see Note,* above), ignore this section and refer to *Trace the design onto the background square* on page 31. Trace all the detail onto the fabric and prepare for embroidery (*see* page 33). The flower and leaf shapes will then be embroidered in two strands of darker pinks and apricots using stem stitch, backstitch, chain-stitch or couching.

In order to minimize confusion when combining fabric shapes with embroidery, each design is explained in the chapter called *Design Details* (pages 43–57). That chapter also gives a list of materials for each design, and refers you back to this chapter for step-by-step instructions.

NOTE
The fabric roses in some of the designs were made to look three-dimensional. This technique, however, is usually used by advanced appliqué artists and does not really form an essential part of these designs. I have shown a quicker, easier method of direct appliqué. If you would like to make the three-dimensional rose shapes, refer to the brief instructions given on page 25.

WHAT DO I NEED?

The exact material requirements are listed under each project. Familiarize yourself with the following sections of the book before beginning, though:
1. *How do I trace and join the quarter and half designs?* (page 8).
2. *Which fabrics and colours do I choose?* (page 9).
3. *How much fabric do I buy?* (page 10).
4. *Which threads and colours do I use?* (page 10).
5. *Why use beads?* (page 11).
6. *Which satin ribbon do I use?* (page 12).
7. *Which batting/wadding do I use?* (page 12).
8. *Why use muslin for backing the batting/wadding?* (page 12).
9. *Which fabric is best for backing cushions and quilts?* (page 12).
10. *Which needles and pins do I use?* (page 13).
11. *Which quilting hoop do I use and why?* (page 13).
12. *Why use a pencil for tracing onto fabric?* (page 13).
13. *Which other materials or equipment do I need?* (page 14).

HINT
Always buy more fabric and embroidery thread than you need in case you run out and you are unable to find what you need of the original dye lot.

ASSEMBLING THE PROJECT

1. Pre-wash the cotton fabrics. Wash 100% cotton fabrics before using, to remove excess printing dyes and because slight shrinkage will occur.
❖ Press the fabric once it is dry.

NOTE
It is unnecessary to wash polysilk fabrics before using, as these do not shrink.

2. Trace the design. Make a tracing of the sections comprising the design and join them.
❖ See *How do I trace and join the quarter and half designs?* (page 8).

3. Make the fabric shapes.

a. Trace the shapes onto the iron-on Vilene or fusible webbing. Turn to your chosen design in the chapter on *Design Details* (pages 43–57).

Turn to your chosen design in the chapter on *Design Details* (pages 43–57).

NOTE

The fabric shapes with all their detail are first drawn onto iron-on Vilene. The Vilene is then ironed onto the fabric. This step ensures a perfectly formed fabric shape.

The instructions for each design will give you a guide to how many shapes to draw, and whether to turn the iron-on Vilene/fusible webbing onto its dull or shiny side when tracing. (The Vilene is sometimes reversed to the dull side when a design uses mirror images of certain shapes. This method is similar to the one followed when tracing and joining the quarter designs.)

Follow the instructions given for each design. Each page containing the relevant shapes for a particular design has been reproduced in full colour to help you avoid confusion with respect to the colours of various shapes.

Using a 3B pencil (with a very soft, dark lead), trace each shape onto the shiny side of the iron-on Vilene/fusible webbing following the instructions on the design. Draw one, two or four of each shape as indicated. Leave spaces between individual shapes and draw neat, sharp lines including all the detail, i.e. the petals, dots and veins of

the leaves *(fig. 1)*. Reverse the iron-on Vilene/fusible webbing and follow the same procedure, now drawing the required number of shapes on its dull side. Always leave a small gap between one shape and the next.

NOTES

❖ *For some designs, e.g.* Harmony, *you will only use the shiny side of the iron-on Vilene/fusible webbing.*

❖ *All the leaves and some flower shapes are labelled for easier identification. Always label the shape on the dull side of the iron-on Vilene/fusible webbing, regardless of which side you have drawn on. Draw the number or letter very lightly as it will not be covered by embroidery stitches and may show through light fabric.*

b. Cut out the Vilene shapes.

i. Do not cut *on* the pencilled line. To prevent fraying, you will only cut along this line once the Vilene has been ironed onto the relevant fabric.

ii. Keep the leaves which are to be ironed onto the same colour fabric together as one unit (cut out so that the shapes remain together in the form of a rectangle or a square). Once ironed onto fabric, cut out the leaves on the pencilled line and keep them together.

iii. For the flowers and bigger shapes follow the pencil line as a guide only – leave a 3–4 mm (⅛ in) edge and cut out each shape *(fig. 2)*.

c. Match the iron-on Vilene/fusible webbing shapes to the correct fabrics.

i. Referring to the chapter on *Design Details* (page 43) for the suggested colour of the shapes, place the correct shape with fabric of the correct colour.

ii. Place the fabric *wrong side up* on the ironing board.

iii. Place the iron-on Vilene/fusible webbing shape *shiny side down* on the wrong side of the fabric.

d. Iron the Vilene/fusible webbing onto the fabric.

i. Carefully set the temperature of the iron to match your chosen fabric.

ii. Iron the silk fabrics first, then reset the iron for cotton fabrics.

iii. Press the iron-on Vilene/fusible webbing onto the wrong side of the fabric so that the heat bonds it.

HINTS

❖ *Only iron on the wrong side of the fabric, as the iron leaves black marks if it has come into contact with the shiny side (glue) of the iron-on Vilene/fusible webbing. If you do find glue on the iron, use a tube of hot iron cleaner (found in most super-markets) to remove it.*

❖ *Check that the iron-on Vilene/fusible webbing has bonded well to the fabric and does not lift along the edges.*

e. Cut out the iron-on Vilene/fusible webbing shapes.

i. Use small, sharp embroidery scissors for precise cutting.

ii. Following the pencil lines on the iron-on Vilene/fusible webbing, cut out each fabric shape as neatly as possible.

f. Trace the pencil detail onto the right side of the fabric.

i. Place each fabric/Vilene shape, fabric side up, against a window or on a glass table with a light underneath.

ii. Use a sharp HB pencil to draw any detail of the shape onto the fabric side of the rose, flower or leaf shape.

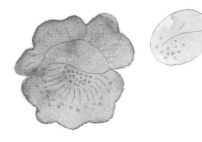

FIG. 1 DRAW EACH SHAPE ONTO THE SHINY OR DULL SIDE OF THE VILENE AS INSTRUCTED

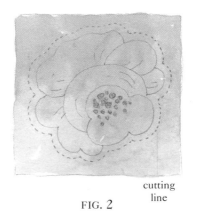

cutting line

FIG. 2

iii. Draw as neatly as possible, and don't draw too thick a line which may show through the embroidery stitches and spoil the work. Do not transfer the number or letter, if any, onto the fabric side of the flower or other shape.

g. Keep the shapes in a small bowl or saucer so that they do not get lost.

4. Cut out the background fabric square.

Choose one of the sizes listed below for the background square.

a. First six designs – *Harmony* to *Solitaire*:

i. For a square that is to be framed: Cut a square of fabric measuring 50 cm x 50 cm (20 in x 20 in) *(fig. 3)*. This size will fit well in a quilting hoop with a diameter of 35.5 cm (14 in). There is no need to draw a smaller square inside the larger one if you will be framing the design.

ii. For a cushion or quilt square: Cut a square of fabric measuring 50 cm x 50 cm (20 in x 20 in). This size will fit well in a quilting hoop with a diameter of 35.5 cm (14 in). Draw a smaller square measuring 40 cm x 40 cm (16 in x 16 in) inside this square *(fig. 4)*. This will be the cutting line once all the embroidery work has been completed.

b. Larger quarter designs – *Rose chain* to *Pompeii* (with the exception of the *Filigree* design):

no need to draw an outline for framing

cut 50 cm x 50 cm (20 in x 20 in)

FIG. 3 FOR FRAMING FIRST SIX DESIGNS: HARMONY TO SOLITAIRE

THE FILIGREE DESIGN IS COMBINED WITH A CORD FINISH ON THIS ROUND CUSHION

i. For a cushion or quilt square without a border: Cut a square of fabric measuring 57 cm x 57 cm (22½ in x 22½ in). This size will fit well in a

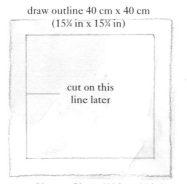

draw outline 40 cm x 40 cm (15¾ in x 15¾ in)

cut on this line later

cut 50 cm x 50 cm (20 in x 20 in)

FIG. 4 CUSHIONS WITH FIRST SIX DESIGNS: HARMONY TO SOLITAIRE

quilting hoop with a diameter of 46 cm (18 in). For a cushion, draw a square measuring 50 cm x 50 cm (20 in x 20 in) inside this square *(fig. 5)*. For a quilt, draw a square measuring 50 cm x 50 cm (20 in x 20 in) or 55 cm x 55 cm (21½ in x 21½ in) inside this square *(fig. 6)*. This will be the cutting line once all the embroidery work has been completed. Refer to the paragraph called *Calculating the number of squares to make up a quilt* (page 37) for more information about the size of squares and other projects. Refer to the instructions for a *Four-block quilt* (page 59) for the size of squares to draw for this particular project.

draw outline
50 cm x 50 cm
(20 in x 20 in)

cut 57 cm x 57 cm (22½ in x 22½ in)

FIG. 5 CUSHION WITHOUT A BORDER:
ROSE CHAIN TO POMPEII

cut 57 cm x 57 cm (22½ in x 22½ in)

draw outline
50 cm x 50 cm
(20 in x 20 in)
OR
55 cm x 55 cm
(21½ in x 21½ in)

FIG. 6 QUILT SQUARE:
ROSE CHAIN TO POMPEII

cut 42 cm x 42 cm (16½ in x 16½ in)

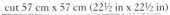

add borders

FIG. 7 CUSHION WITH A COLOURED
BORDER: ROSE CHAIN TO CAMROSE

cut 52 cm x 52 cm (20½ in x 20½ in)

draw outline
40 cm x 40 cm
(15¾ in x 15¾ in)
or smaller depending
on size required

FIG. 8 BABY'S QUILT OR SMALLER QUILT
SQUARES: TEGAN-L TO GUYLIN-V

ii. For a cushion with a coloured border (e.g. the *Monarch* design): Cut a square measuring 42 cm x 42 cm (16½ in x 16½ in) *(fig. 7)*. There is no need to draw a smaller square inside. Referring to step 9 on page 32, cut and attach the border strips. The square with the attached border will need to have strips of scrap fabric added to it in order to be large enough to fit in a quilting hoop with a diameter of 46 cm (18 in) *(see* step 10, *Place the layers of fabric together and position them in a quilting hoop,* on page 32).

c. Six smaller designs: *Tegan-L* to *Guylin-V* designs for making the *Six-block baby's quilt* (page 60).

For a baby's quilt or for making smaller quilt squares: Cut a square of fabric measuring 52 cm x 52 cm (20½ in x 20½ in). This size will fit well into a quilting hoop with a diameter of 41 cm (16 in). Draw a smaller square inside. Choose a square measuring from 40 cm x 40 cm (15¾ in x 15¾ in) to 32 cm x 32 cm (12½ in x 12½ in) depending on the size you prefer. This will be the cutting line once all the embroidery work has been completed.

d. Smallest designs for various other projects: Refer to the chapter called *Other projects* (page 59) for specific instructions on the *Bridesmaid's dress* (page 62).

NOTES

❖ *The batting/wadding and muslin squares will be cut to measure the same size as the background square.*

❖ *When making squares for a quilt, it is very important that all the squares (the original squares and the squares indicating cutting lines) are measured accurately. If the squares differ in size, they will not line up neatly when joined. To ensure consistent sizing, I recommend making a cardboard template (fig. 9). The outline of the cardboard square should be*

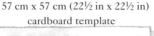

57 cm x 57 cm (22½ in x 22½ in)
cardboard template

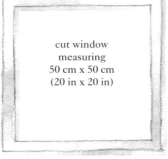

cut window
measuring
50 cm x 50 cm
(20 in x 20 in)

FIG. 9 MAKE A CARDBOARD TEMPLATE

the same size as the first (larger) fabric square required, e.g. 57 cm x 57 cm (22½ in x 22½ in). Draw and cut a window (smaller square) inside the larger outline to indicate the eventual cutting line, e.g. 50 cm x 50 cm (20 in x 20 in).

6. Pin the design to the background fabric square.

a. Taking the sheet of paper with your chosen design on it, make sure that the design is positioned squarely. Cut off the excess paper to make it square if necessary. Check that the designs drawn to size are positioned centrally on the sheet of paper.

b. Place the square of background fabric, right side up, on top of the right side of the design. The cream or light-coloured fabric will allow the design to show through easily.

c. Position the design centrally on the fabric square. Pin the paper to the fabric at the four corners of the design and along all four sides of the paper *(figs. 10a* and *10b)*.

d. Ensure that the fabric is lying smoothly and avoid any creases.

e. If you have chosen a dark background fabric (e.g. green) and you are unable to see the design through the fabric, try taping the design and fabric square to a sunny window or onto a glass table with a light underneath it. The design should show through.

As a last resort you could make a tracing of the design on tracing paper. Place the tracing paper on top of the background fabric and slip the Vilened shapes underneath the tracing paper to guide you when gluing shapes to the background fabric.

7. Glue and position the fabric shapes onto the background square.

a. Take a numbered leaf shape, note the number, and, using the glue stick, cover the wrong side (Vilene/webbing side) of the leaf with glue. Pay special attention to the edges. (Use scraps of paper under your work when gluing to avoid a sticky work surface).

b. Take the glued leaf, and note the number on it that shows through the background fabric. Some of the numbers will be reversed. (If you are unable to see the number clearly

drawn outline

FIG. 10A JOINED QUARTER DESIGN
PINNED CENTRALLY

FIG. 10B PIN PAPER TO FABRIC

FIG. 11 GLUE AND POSITION FABRIC
SHAPES ON BACKGROUND FABRIC

through the fabric, refer to the design in the book as a guide.) Now glue each leaf onto the background fabric. Press each glued leaf down onto the fabric over the leaf with the corresponding number on the design. Press down well, especially around the edges.

NOTE

There is an extra seam added onto some of the leaves. This is because the leaf will fit underneath the adjoining shape.

c. Take the flower shapes and glue them to the background fabric as explained above. Use the shape of the flower as a guide for positioning if the flower is not labelled. (If you are using puffed, three-dimensional rose shapes (*see* page 25), remember to apply glue to only the centre of each rose.

e. The fabric leaves and flowers have now all been positioned and glued to the background fabric *(fig. 11)*.

f. Do not remove the pins yet.

8. Trace the design onto the background square.

a. Taking a sharp HB pencil, *lightly* and neatly trace the remaining detail of the design onto the background

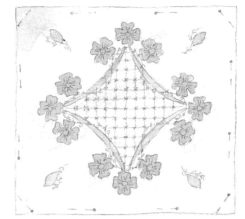

FIG. 12 LIGHTLY TRACE REMAINING
DETAIL ONTO BACKGROUND FABRIC

fabric square (*see fig. 12* and *Important Note* at the bottom of this page).

b. For some of the designs, draw an X where each ribbon rose is to be attached, draw all the flower stems, embroidery stitch shapes and any outline of the design.

NOTE

The larger teardrop shapes on the design are to be stitched in silk ribbon. Draw these shapes smaller than shown on the design. This will ensure that the pencil line does not show beyond the shape formed by the silk ribbon stitches.

c. For the quarter and the half designs, draw any straight lines or squares *using a ruler*. Draw any other lines or shapes not covered by the fabric shapes.

IMPORTANT NOTE

Draw lightly – the pencil lines will be more prominent once the square is placed on the batting/wadding in the hoop. Never draw a second (i.e. double) line if you made a mistake the first time. The mistake will not be noticed, but a double line will! Pencil marks do not rub out, wash out or fade with time. The lines will therefore not disappear, but as they are covered by embroidery stitches (even the quilting/running stitch) they disappear as you sew. The pencilled lines must therefore not be too thick (use a sharp pencil) or too dark (draw lightly).

d. All the details of the design have now been transferred onto the background fabric.

e. Remove all the pins and the paper design now.

9. Attach the border strips. Ignore this step if you are making a square to be framed, a cushion without borders or a square for a quilt.

a. Choose suitable fabric for the border strips.

❖ A border is like a frame and should complement and enhance the design, outlining the decorated square as an individual piece of art.

❖ Use border strips made of the same fabric as the flowers or leaves that you would like to emphasize, or choose floral or patterned fabric if you like. Using the same colour borders as the background fabric can be a little dull.

b. Cut out the border strips.

i. Take the rectangular strip of fabric measuring 57 cm x 24 cm (22½ in x 9½ in) (*see Which other materials or equipment do I need?* on page 14) and cut it into four strips, each measuring 6 cm (2¼ in) in width. If you prefer, fold the rectangle in half lengthwise, press with a hot iron, fold in half again and press. Unfold and cut along the folded lines to obtain four identical strips.

ii. Shorten two of the strips to about 42 cm (16½ in) in length, i.e. the length of the fabric square (*see* strips marked 1 and 2 on *fig. 14a* and *Hint*, below).

HINT
I always cut these shortened strips 2–3 cm (¾–1¼ in) longer than required, just in case I have miscalculated.

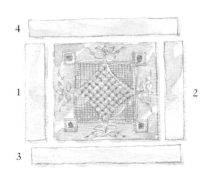

FIG. 14A

c. Stitch to attach the border strips.

i. With right sides together, pin the background square and one of the shortened border strips together along the edge (*see* strip 1 on fig. 14b). Insert the pins as shown, or tack the border and the square together.

ii. Stitch the strip and the background square together by machine, working 6 mm (¼ in) from the raw edge of the square. Sew over the pins or remove them as you stitch.

iii. Repeat this procedure along the opposite side of the background square, using the other shortened strip.

iv. Press the seams flat on the wrong side so that they lie towards the border fabric *(fig. 14c)* – check the temperature of your iron!

v. Now attach the two longer strips to the remaining two sides of the square, stitching the borders together at each end *(fig. 14d)*.

vi. Press the seams to lie towards the border fabric, as before.

FIG. 14C PRESS ON WRONG SIDE

FIG. 14B PIN FIRST TWO BORDER STRIPS INTO POSITION

10. Place the layers of fabric together and position them in a quilting hoop.

a. Take a square of batting/wadding which has been cut to the same size as the background square. If you are making a cushion with a border, cut the batting/wadding to measure 57 cm x 57 cm (22½ in x 22½ in). This batting square needs to be slightly larger to allow for the shrinkage which will occur during the quilting process.

b. Cut a muslin square to the same size as the batting/wadding.

c. Lay the muslin square flat on your work surface.

d. Lay the batting/wadding square on top of the muslin. The least fluffy side of the batting/wadding should face down (against the muslin).

e. Position the background square centrally on top of the batting/wadding (*see* figs. 15 and 16 on page 33). Check each layer of the fabric 'sandwich', carefully smoothing out any creases.

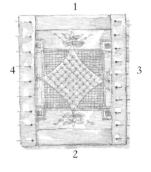

FIG. 14D PIN LAST TWO BORDER STRIPS INTO POSITION

add on fabric strips if necessary

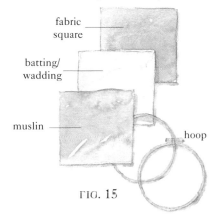

fabric square

batting/ wadding

muslin

hoop

FIG. 15

NOTE

If you are making a cushion square with a border, you may need to add fabric strips to enlarge your square in order to ensure a good fit in the 46 cm (18 in) quilting hoop before laying the fabric on top of the batting/wadding (fig. 15).

f. There is no need to tack the various layers together when using a hoop. The layers cannot move once tautly positioned in the hoop.

g. Take a hoop measuring either 35.5 cm (14 in), 41 cm (16 in) or 46 cm (18 in) (*see Which quilting hoop do I use and why?* on page 13). Place the three-layered fabric 'sandwich' into the hoop as follows *(fig. 16)*:

i. Place the inner hoop centrally under the muslin.

ii. Unscrew the wing nut to open/ enlarge the outer frame.

iii. Place the outer frame centrally over the background fabric.

iv. Squeeze the outer hoop over the inner one. (It helps to work on the floor using one knee as a 'third hand'.)

v. Tighten the wing nut halfway and stretch the top layer of fabric until it is quite taut.

vi. Tighten/pull on the muslin at the back until it too, is taut. Never pull on the batting/wadding, though, as it tears rather easily.

vii. The fabrics should now be smooth, but not stretched to the extent that the shape of the pencilled design has been distorted.

viii. Tighten the wing nut to secure the layers of fabric in the hoop.

HINTS

❖ *The various layers of fabric do loosen a little as you work. Remember to tighten all the layers by pulling the top fabric taut along the raw edges every time you pick up the hoop to start again. A perfectly smooth article will ensure a good finish with no puckering.*

❖ *It is important to make sure that any creases in the background fabric are ironed out before placing the layers of fabric in the hoop. Remember that a quilted article cannot be pressed later. If it is pressed, the effect of the quilting will be spoiled.*

ix. Roll up the four corners outside the hoop and pin or tack them in position so that the bulkiness of the layers of muslin, batting/wadding and background fabric do not hinder you while you are embroidering.

11. Embroider the design.

a. Prepare for embroidery.

i. Refer to *Which threads and colours do I use?* (page 10), *Which needles and pins do I use?* (page 13) and *Hints when embroidering* (page 14).

ii. Refer to the chapter called *Design Details* (page 43) for a guide to colours and materials to use for each design.

iii. Refer to the embroidery stitch codes and legends on pages 20–21 and the stitch guides on pages 17–20.

USING EMBROIDERY THREAD

❖ Never cut a thread longer than from the tip of a finger to 10 cm (4 in) above the elbow (no more than 50 cm [20 in]), otherwise it will knot. You will have to use a longer thread for couching stitches, though.

USING SILK RIBBON

❖ Silk ribbon 3–4 mm (⅛ in) wide is combined with embroidery thread to enhance the designs, adding another dimension to the work.

❖ To maintain a balanced design, use silk ribbon for only some (not all) of the embroidery stitches, for example:

– To make French knots or colonial knots. Wind once around the needle.

– To make extended knots. Wind once around the needle.

– To make a detached chain or larger lazy daisies.

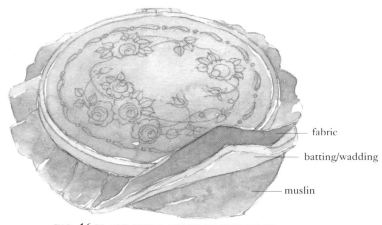

fabric

batting/wadding

muslin

FIG. 16 PLACE THE LAYERS IN THE HOOP

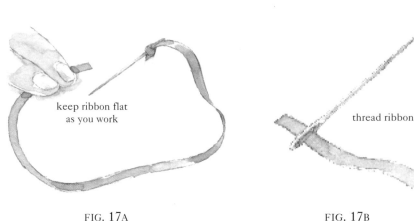

FIG. 17A

keep ribbon flat
as you work

thread ribbon

FIG. 17B

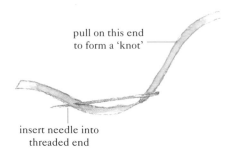

pull on this end
to form a 'knot'

insert needle into
threaded end

FIG. 17C

❖ Keep the silk ribbon flat and as untwisted as possible as you work (*fig. 17a*). Gently pull the ribbon through the different layers of fabric as you work, so that it does not become tatty and spoil the effect.

❖ Thread the needle as follows:

– Insert the ribbon through the eye of the chenille needle (*fig. 17b*).

– Push the sharp point of the needle into the short, threaded end of the ribbon (*fig. 17c*).

– Pull the long tail of the ribbon to tighten the 'knot'. Threading the ribbon in this way means that it cannot be pulled out of the eye of the needle. In addition, you will be able to work with very short lengths, thus saving on the amount of silk ribbon you use.

HINTS WHEN WORKING WITH SILK RIBBON

❖ *Cut the ribbon into lengths measuring approximately 30–40 cm (12–15 in). If the length of ribbon you are working with is too long, it will become tatty and it may even tear after a while.*

❖ *Start and end off your work with a short tail of ribbon that can be caught in the next stitch. A knot tied in the ribbon is bulky and may loosen in time.*

❖ *Use a no. 22 chenille needle for silk ribbon work – a needle with a small eye causes the ribbon to fold.*

❖ *When cutting silk ribbon, cut it at an angle to form a sharp point which will make it easier to thread.*

BEFORE BEGINNING TO EMBROIDER YOUR CHOSEN DESIGN, TAKE NOTE

❖ For a better finish, embroider the tightest stitches first. Follow the order given here: quilting or running stitch, backstitch, stem stitch, couching, satin stitch, chain stitch, honeycomb, detached chain, lazy daisy, French or colonial knot, lastly adding the beads.

❖ Most of the embroidery stitches are made through all three layers (muslin, batting/wadding and fabric). The exceptions are chain stitch, detached chain, lazy daisies, couching and honeycomb, which are only *anchored* through all the layers.

❖ It does not matter where you start embroidering. Without a hoop you would have to start in the centre of the design and work outwards. Once taut in the hoop, however, the layers cannot move.

❖ Pull each stitch as tight as possible as you sew. This means that all the stitches will create a quilted effect by anchoring the layers of fabric together. The only stitches that will not be tightened as you sew, are the chain stitches and detached chains.

❖ The stitches suggested are merely guidelines. More experienced needle-workers may wish to be more creative, using different, more elaborate stitches.

b. Start embroidery.
If you have decided not to use fabric shapes, and are using only embroidery

stitches to make up the design, embroider the flower and leaf shapes using two strands of embroidery thread and stem stitch, backstitch and chain stitch or couching. Use darker shades of pink or peach thread. (*See* step iii at the top of page 35 for embroidering the remaining detail of the design).

i. Anchor the fabric shapes.
Start by anchoring the glued fabric shapes to the background fabric first to prevent the raw edges from fraying.

– Use two strands of matching embroidery thread and a quilting or running stitch about 1 mm (a fraction of an inch) away from the raw edge of the fabric shape.

For articles that are to be framed, the quilting or running stitch is adequate. The raw edges will not fray, as the item is never washed (*fig. 18a*).

– For any article that will be washed, such as a cushion or quilt, use a chain stitch to cover the quilting or running stitch and the raw edges of

use quilting or running stitches along raw edges

FIG. 18A FOR FRAMED ARTICLES

cover quilting stitch with chain stitch
or couching along raw edges

FIG. 18B FOR ARTICLES TO BE WASHED

the fabric shapes *(fig. 18b)*. Use two strands of thread for this chain. Alternatively, you may like to cover the raw edge of the shape using couching in six strands of thread, anchored with two strands of thread in the same colour.

HINTS

❖ *You may find it easier to make the chain stitches right at the end when the work has been removed from the hoop. First quilt around the raw edge. Complete all the embroidery, quilting and the ribbon roses. Then remove the work from the hoop and make the chain stitches around the raw edges of the leaves and the other shapes.*

❖ *If you have chosen couching to cover the raw edges, this is easier sewn when all the layers are still in the hoop.*

❖ *Here is an interesting alternative to chain stitches or couching. Use two strands of embroidery thread and anchor the fabric shapes along the raw edge with French or colonial knots. Anchor the shapes through all layers of fabric. Start by making a French or colonial knot just on the edge of the fabric shape and proceed along the shape so that the raw edge of the fabric is covered by the knots. Make one, two or even three rows of knots close together (fig. 19).*

EMBROIDERING THE DETAIL ON THE FABRIC FLOWER AND LEAF SHAPES

❖ Use two strands of embroidery thread in a shade darker than the fabric

flower or leaf shape, e.g. use rose pink thread for a dusty pink flower shape, or darker green thread on a lighter green fabric leaf shape.

❖ Make a knot at the long end and bring the needle and thread upwards from the back of the work, through all the layers including the fabric flower. The needle should protrude from a point along one of the pencilled lines.

❖ Use a backstitch or stem stitch to embroider along the pencilled lines so that the flower detail is made.

❖ Add beads to the centre of the flower (*see Attaching a bead* on page 20). The beads are sewn on through all the layers of fabric. Pull the thread tight so that the beads lie snugly on the flower.

❖ Embroider French or colonial knots in-between and along the edge of the beadwork to soften the outline *(fig. 20)*. French or colonial knots are also embroidered at the ends of any stamens of the flower centre.

❖ Use a large quilting or running stitch or a backstitch in the same colour to create any stamens on the rose. Use either one or two strands of thread.

❖ Embroider the veins of the leaves very carefully as well. Stitch through all the layers of fabric, using two strands of thread (one strand on very small shapes) and backstitch or stem stitch. Quilting stitch or running stitch

may also be used. Stitch along the pencilled lines through all the layers of fabric, pulling the stitches tight.

iii. Embroider the remaining detail of the design on the background square. Refer to the *Stitch codes and legends* (page 21) and to your chosen design for a guide to the colours and stitches to use, and to *Which threads and colours do I use?* (page 10).

– Quilt any square blocks on the design using two strands of thread.

– Use couching or chain stitch, backstitch or stem stitch to form any circular outlines on the design.

– Refer to the design for a guide to which other stitches to use.

HINTS

❖ *Check the background fabric carefully to see that all the pencil marks have been covered before removing the work from the hoop. Add beads where indicated.*

❖ *Look at the work in the embroidery hoop in a mirror to get a good idea of what the finished product will look like. Add extra embroidery stitches, beads or silk ribbon until you are satisfied with the effect.*

❖ *Blue thread is really effective to 'lift' the colours on a busy design (e.g. Harmony). Use two strands of medium or light blue thread, and make French or colonial knots in-between the other stitches.*

FIG. 19 USE CLOSE FRENCH OR COLONIAL KNOTS ALONG RAW EDGE

FIG. 20 FRENCH OR COLONIAL KNOTS AND BEADS

PREPARING INDIVIDUAL SQUARES FOR MAKING UP A CUSHION OR QUILT

1. Place the quilted square right side down on an ironing board so that the fabric background is face down and the muslin side is showing.

2. Make sure that you set your iron to the correct temperature. Lift the loose sections of the muslin and batting/wadding layers to expose the wrong side of the background fabric square. First test the temperature of the iron on a corner of the wrong side of the background fabric *(fig. 21)*.

3. Now press the wrong side of the loose sections of the background fabric square where it has creased in the hoop and at the four corners.

4. Turn the square right side up (i.e. with the muslin layer at the bottom) and pin the background fabric to the batting/wadding. Insert the pins at right angles to the edge along the pencilled line *(fig. 22)*.

5. Place the pins 2.5–3 cm (1–1¼ in) apart so that the unpinned fabric will not make a fold as you zigzag the edge.

6. Use a wide zigzag stitch that is set so that the stitches are not too far apart, and zigzag along the pencilled line through all the layers. (I sew over the pins, but you may wish to remove them as you sew.)

7. Remove the pins and cut just outside the zigzagged edge to remove the excess fabric, batting/wadding and muslin. If you have cut the zigzag stitches in places by mistake, simply zigzag over the loose edges again.

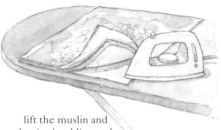

lift the muslin and batting/wadding and press wrong side of fabric

FIG. 21

pencilled line

pin at right angles to edge along pencilled line

backing fabric

FIG. 22

BORDEAUX (LEFT) AND HARMONY (RIGHT), BOTH USING PUFFED, THREE-DIMENSIONAL SHAPES, HAVE BEEN GIVEN BEAUTIFUL FRAMES

FINISHING A CUSHION

There are several different ways of finishing a cushion. As most readers are probably familiar with the methods involved, I have, in the interest of space, concentrated on explaining how to prepare the squares for embroidery and how to make up the designs. Choose a lace or frill finish for bedroom cushions and a binding or cord finish for lounge cushions. Please refer to the section on attaching binding (page 40) – the *Six-block baby's quilt* (page 6) uses the same width binding as a cushion.

Binding is stitched on by machine, right sides together, folded over to the back of the work, and stitched onto the backing by hand *(fig. 23)*.

Decorative cord is sewn on by hand once the cushion has been made up and filled. Start and end the cording by inserting a tail of 4–5 cm (1½–2 in) of cord at one corner that has been opened (just snip the stitching to open the corner) *(fig. 24)*.

CALCULATING THE NUMBER OF SQUARES TO MAKE UP A QUILT

This information applies to a quilt without sashing (borders). Sashing is extra work and not essential for these designs. A cord or lace finish, added after the quilt squares have been joined, serves a similar function to sashing, but it is far easier to apply.

NOTE
The following information applies to the larger, quarter designs, e.g. from the Rose Chain *design to the* Pompeii *design.*

❖ Refer to the earlier sections on *Which fabrics and colours do I choose?* (page 9) and to *How much fabric do I buy?* (page 10).

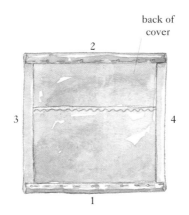

back of cover

FIG. 23 FINISHING WITH BINDING

❖ Most silky fabrics are 115 cm (45 in) wide. You will be able to make roughly four squares from 1.25 m (1¼ yds).

❖ Cut *all* the quilt squares to measure 57 cm x 57 cm (22½ in x 22½ in) so that each square will fit snugly into the 46 cm (18 in) quilting hoop. This ensures that the entire design to be embroidered will fit inside the hoop. You will therefore not have to reposition the hoop to embroider different sections of the design. Draw a smaller square, the size of which is calculated according to the size of your mattress, on each quilt square (*see* step 4, *Cut out the background fabric square*, on page 29).

NOTE
Instructions for the smaller Six-block baby's quilt *are given in the section called* Other Projects *on page 60.*

❖ Draw a square measuring one of the following sizes inside each 57 cm x 57 cm (22½ in x 22½ in) square:

a. For a single, twin, double or standard king-size mattress, draw an inner square measuring 50 cm x 50 cm (20 in x 20 in).

b. For a queen-size or extra-long king-size mattress, draw an inner square measuring 55 cm x 55 cm (22 in x 22 in).

– This inner square will only be edged and cut down to size once all the embroidery work has been completed.

– Always use an HB or B pencil to draw the lines onto the fabric and a T-square to ensure that you draw a perfect square for each block.

Estimate how many squares you will need for your particular quilt. Please measure the exact size of your mattress and adjust the given measurements accordingly (*see A guide to mattress sizes* on page 14). As all the quilt blocks are square, you will need to improvise and adjust the measurements according to the quilt size you require (so that it will fit the length and width of your particular mattress neatly).

HINTS
❖ *Use a cardboard template when marking out squares for quilt-making, as all the squares need to be exactly the same size (see* Notes *and fig. 9 on page 30).*

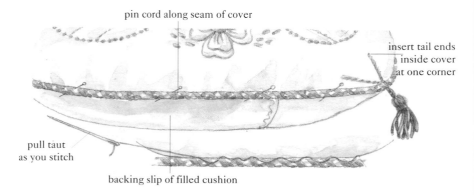

pin cord along seam of cover

insert tail ends inside cover at one corner

pull taut as you stitch

backing slip of filled cushion

FIG. 24

add extra rows of squares for overhang

FIG. 25

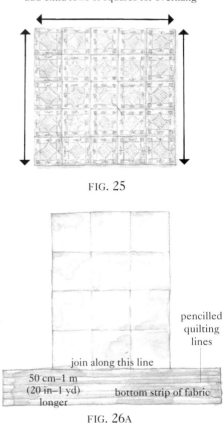

FIG. 26A

FIG. 26B

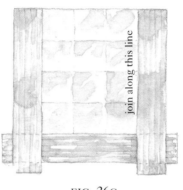

FIG. 26C

❖ *Always buy an extra metre (yard) or two of fabric when planning a quilt. The dye lots of the fabric may differ if you run out and have to buy extra fabric at a later date. Extra fabric can always be used to make cushions, tie-backs for curtains, or even a tablecloth.*

How much fabric do I need?

❖ Do your calculations based on four squares per 1.25 m (1¼ yds) (*see How much fabric do I buy?* on page 10).

❖ You will need extra fabric for the sides or overhang of the quilt. Two extra rows of squares can be joined to the squares that lie on the top surface of the bed. An extra row of squares will also be joined along the bottom of the quilt to allow for the overhang at the bottom of the bed (*fig. 25*).

❖ Alternatively, you may prefer to add long strips of fabric and batting/wadding to the sides of the quilt to allow for the overhang. These strips are joined to the embroidered squares and quilted lengthwise (*figs. 26a, 26b, 26c and 26d*). This method saves the time and expense of making extra rows of squares. This method requires about 6 m (6½ yds) of additional fabric.

JOINING THE SQUARES TO MAKE UP THE QUILT

Refer to *Preparing individual squares for making up a cushion or quilt* on page 36. Each square will be prepared following these instructions before it is joined to other squares. It is essential that all the squares are exactly the same size to ensure that the seams will be perfectly aligned when the squares are joined.

❖ Individual squares are first joined to form rows (*fig. 27*). Thereafter, one row is joined to the next (*fig. 27*).

1. Lay the decorated squares on a table or on the floor and arrange your design. Lay out the squares in two rows (three or four rows for larger quilts).

2. With rights sides together, pin one square to another, positioning the pins at right angles to the edge (*fig. 28*). You will stitch over the pins later. Add the adjoining squares in the same row so that all the squares making up that row are pinned together, with right sides together. Match up the corners, then ease the centre to line up the blocks.

FIG. 26D

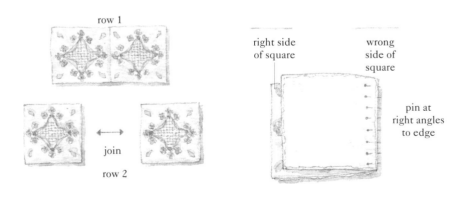

FIG. 27 JOIN SQUARES TO FORM ROWS

FIG. 28

❖ *Always open out joined squares before pinning additional adjoining ones into place. In this way you will ensure that no square is upside down.*

❖ *Arrange the decorated squares so that the round designs are placed in the centre, for example, and the square designs in the corners. Another option, in the case of larger quilts, is to place the busiest designs in the centre and at the corners. The quilt design must look balanced overall – too many heavy or busy designs on one side will result in a lopsided look.*

3. Keeping the right sides together, machine stitch to join two squares at a time, leaving a seam of 1 cm (⅜ in) and stitching through all six layers of fabric. Stitch all the squares together in this way to form two, three or even four rows, depending on the size of your quilt. Remove the pins.

4. Lay the rows of squares out on the table or floor, right side up. Make sure that the rows are arranged as planned previously. It is very easy to turn a row upside down inadvertently when joining it to others.

5. Pin the rows of squares together, with right sides together, placing the pins at right angles to the edges *(fig. 29)*. Machine stitch to join rows, leaving a seam of 1 cm (⅜ in) and stitching through all six layers as before.

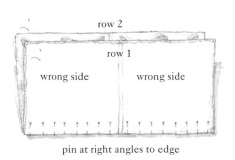

FIG. 29 JOIN ROWS OF SQUARES

FIG. 30 ATTACH THE BACKING

6. Remove all the pins, open up the quilt and place it wrong side up on a large table or on the floor.

ATTACHING THE BACKING

Begin by referring to the section called *Which fabric is best for backing cushions and quilts?* on page 12. Remember that the backing fabric is always cut larger than the quilt squares or the cushion square to allow for possible stretching of the quilted squares when the layers are stitched together.

1. Pin the pressed sheet or backing fabric which you have chosen to the joined squares, wrong sides together. Pin from the centre, working outwards to the edges, pinning at right angles to the edge of the quilt.

2. In the case of larger quilts, you may wish to *tack* the backing fabric to the muslin and batting/wadding. Tacking is unnecessary for the small *Four-block quilt* (page 59) or the equally small *Six-block baby's quilt* (page 60) – the pins are adequate to hold the layers together. Remember to leave the backing fabric wider all round than the quilt – do not trim the excess fabric from the edges at this stage.

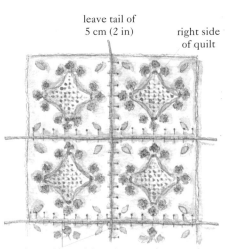

FIG. 31 ADD CORD TO FINISH

3. Turn the quilt to the right side and pin along the zigzagged edge. Pin at right angles to the edge, with 3–5 cm (1¼–2 in) between pins *(fig. 30)*.

4. Follow the inside of the zigzagged stitches on the quilt and straight stitch through all four layers of fabric. Remove the pins as you sew.

5. Carefully remove all the pins from both sides of the quilt and cut off the excess backing fabric.

ADDING LACE OR CORD (OPTIONAL)

Some people like using either lace or cushion cord as a decorative feature in the grooves that are formed when the quilted squares are joined.

❖ Cord or lace, sewn on by hand, is highly effective to enhance and finish the quilt professionally. It is quite acceptable, though, to leave the quilt free of lace or cord if you prefer. I have used a cord finish on both the wall quilt and the baby's quilt illustrated in this book. Pin the cord vertically and horizontally along the grooves of the quilt, leaving a tail of about 5 cm (2 in) at the beginning and the end each time *(fig. 31)*.

NOTE
*Whipstitch the cord tails when starting and
ending to prevent unravelling.*

*– The cord is couched onto the quilt. The
cord is the substitute for the six strands of
thread and is anchored to the quilt with four
strands of matching embroidery thread (see
Couching on page 20).*

*– To create a decorative lace finish, pin
and sew the lace down along each edge of
the lace to anchor it to the quilt. Use
running stitch, backstitch, or a blind hemstitch. The stitches are only sewn through the
lace, fabric and a fraction of the batting/
wadding. Do not sew through all the
layers. Leave a 5 cm (2 in) tail of lace at
each edge of the quilt. These tails will be
tucked in when the binding is attached.*

ATTACHING THE BINDING
TO THE EDGES OF THE QUILT
OR CUSHION

There is no hard and fast rule about
the width of the binding for a quilt.
The width varies according to the size
of the quilt you are making. For the
cushions, *Four-block quilt* and *Six-block
baby's quilt* I cut the binding strips
4–6 cm (1½–2¼ in) wide. Once stitched
and folded, the binding is 1½–2 cm
(½–¾ in) wide. For larger quilts I
recommend using binding that is cut
13 cm (5 in) wide. Once folded, it will
be about 6 cm (2¼ in) wide.

1. Make the binding.

There is no need to cut the fabric
strips on the bias to make the binding
for these quilts or scatter cushions. In
fact, the fabric puckers less if it is not
cut on the bias.

❖ When choosing fabric for making the
binding, consider using a contrasting
colour which blends well with your
general colour scheme.

❖ Calculate how much fabric you will
need to make the binding using the
following instructions as a guide. Take

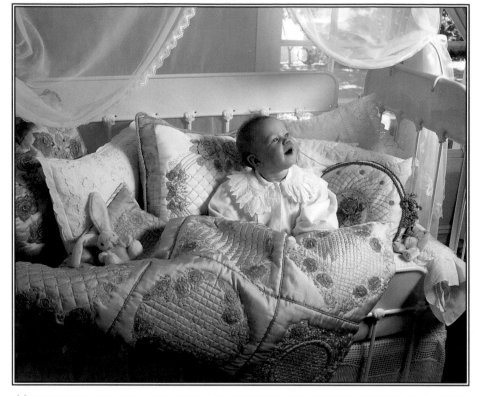

NARROW CORD HAS BEEN USED IN THE GROOVES BETWEEN SQUARES OF THE BABY'S QUILT

the *Six-block baby's quilt* (page 60) as
an example, using binding that is about
4 cm (1½ in) wide. Measure one long
side of the quilt. The quilt may be
102 cm (40 in) long, which means that
you can cut binding strips along the
width of the fabric. (The fabric is
usually at least 115 cm [45 in] wide.)
You will need four binding strips
per quilt. This means that you will
need a total of 16 cm (6 in) of fabric
(i.e. 4 cm x 4 [1½ in x 4]. To make

binding for the *Four-block quilt* on
page 59 you will require more or less
the same amount of fabric.

a. Mark out four strips, each
measuring 4 cm (1½ in) in width, across
the full width of the fabric.

b. Cut the fabric into strips along
the lines that you have drawn.

c. Use a tin of spray starch (available from most supermarkets) to assist
you further. Spray the starch onto the
wrong side of one strip of fabric. Fold

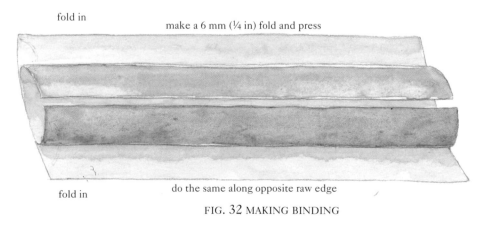

fold in

make a 6 mm (¼ in) fold and press

fold in

do the same along opposite raw edge

FIG. 32 MAKING BINDING

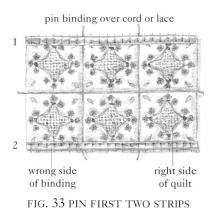

pin binding over cord or lace

wrong side
of binding

right side
of quilt

FIG. 33 PIN FIRST TWO STRIPS

open binding outwards

open binding outwards, right side up

FIG. 34 PIN REMAINING TWO STRIPS

over 6 mm (¼ in) to the wrong side along each long side (raw edge) of the strip (*fig. 32*). Press.

e. Now fold the folded strip in half, with the folded edges together and the wrong side on the inside. Press.

f. Repeat this procedure with each of the remaining three strips.

2. Attach the four binding strips to the front of the quilt.

a. Unfold a strip of binding. Place the binding along one long side of the quilt, with right sides together. The raw edge of the binding should lie on top of the zigzagged edge of the quilt.

b. Pin the binding to the quilt, placing the pins at right angles to the raw edge, and about 2–3 cm (¾–1½ in) apart (*fig. 33*). Pin the binding over the decorative lace or cord (if you have used any) on the quilt.

c. Repeat this procedure to attach the second binding strip, working on the side opposite the first (*fig. 33*).

d. Machine stitch through all five layers along the first pressed fold on the binding, i.e. the fold nearest to the edge of the quilt. Stitch over the pins or remove them as you go. Stitch over any cord or lace. Remove the pins.

e. Fold both the attached binding strips over along the stitching line so that the right sides are facing up.

f. Now pin the third binding strip into position along one of the short sides of the quilt, using the same

method as before, but pinning from the raw edge of binding strip 1 to the raw edge of binding strip 2 (*fig. 34*).

h. Repeat this procedure to pin the fourth binding strip into position along the remaining side of the quilt.

i. Machine stitch through all five layers to attach the two binding strips, using the same method as before. Remove all the pins.

3. Attach the binding to the backing. Turn the quilt over so that the backing is showing and fold the binding over to the back of the quilt. Cut off the excess cord or lace, neatly folding the remainder in to lie inside the binding strips. Hemstitch in place (*figs. 35a and 35b*).

ADAPTING THESE DESIGNS FOR OTHER CRAFTS

The designs which I have included in this book are extremely versatile. They can be adapted for the following crafts:

1. Machine appliqué
2. Candlewicking and quilting

a. Trace the design onto the background fabric square using an HB pencil (*see* step 8, *Trace the design onto the background square*, on page 31).

b. Place the layers of fabric in a quilting hoop (*see Which quilting hoop do I use and why?* on page 13, and *Place the layers of fabric together and position them in a quilting hoop* on page 32).

c. Embroider the design through all the layers (*see* step 11, *Embroider the design*, on page 33 and step b, *Start embroidery*, on page 34).

3. Shadow work
These designs are highly suitable for shadow appliqué and quilting.

4. Dressmaking
Use sections of the designs, e.g. the roses and fabric leaves of *Bordeaux* or the complete small designs in this book (pages 91–94) to adorn T-shirts, jerseys and dresses. Refer to the sections in the book from *Make the fabric shapes* (page 28) to step 8, *Trace the design onto the background square* (page 31). The fabric shapes are glued onto the shirt, jersey or dress and anchored to the background using chain stitch, or buttonhole stitch.

5. Making gifts
Adorn tissue box covers, tea cosies, tray cloths and place mats using ribbon roses or sections of these designs for appliqué or embroidery work.

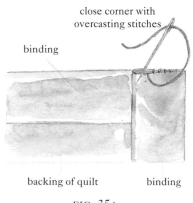

close corner with
overcasting stitches

binding

backing of quilt   binding

FIG. 35A

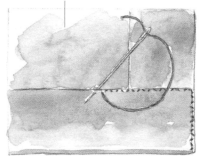

backing of quilt

pull thread so that stitches are hidden

FIG. 35B

DESIGN DETAILS

This chapter links the step-by-step instructions in the previous chapter to the designs supplied in the final section of the book. Here each design is discussed individually and in detail. You will find a list of the materials required, as well as additional notes on the method to be used to complete each design. Use these notes in conjunction with the step-by-step instructions to which you will be referred each time and study the labels that accompany the illustrations. It is a good idea to read through all the instructions for a particular design first, though you may want to begin sewing immediately!

HARMONY

Materials

– IRON-ON VILENE OR FUSIBLE WEBBING: a strip of 10 cm (4 in) (*see* pages 14 and 28)

– ROSES: 20 cm x 9 cm (8 in x 3½ in) of pink fabric (*see Which colours and textures do I use for fabric shapes?* on page 9)

– LEAVES: 18 cm x 7 cm (7 in x 2¾ in) of green fabric (*see* page 9)

– BACKGROUND SQUARE: 50 cm x 50 cm (20 in x 20 in) of cream fabric (*see Which colours do I use for fabric backgrounds?* on page 9)

– BATTING/WADDING: a square measuring 55 cm x 55 cm (22 in x 22 in) (*see* page 12)

– MUSLIN: a square measuring 55 cm x 55 cm (22 in x 22 in) (*see* page 12 if you will be framing the article)

– FOR EMBROIDERY: (*see Which threads and colours do I use?* on page 10)

a. one skein of six-strand embroidery thread in each of the following colours: green, pink, white and blue

b. silk ribbon in three colours: 2 m (2¼ yds) yellow, 1–2 m (1–2¼ yds) light pink, 4 m (4½ yds) green

– SATIN RIBBON ROSES: satin ribbon (*see* pages 12 and 22–24) in four colours: 2 x 12 cm (5 in) apricot, 4 x 12 cm (5 in) dusty pink, 3 x 12 cm (5 in) lighter pink, 1 x 12 cm (5 in) yellow (i.e. a total of ten lengths)

– BEADS: one packet of dusty pink or darker pink beads (*see* page 11)

Method

1. Follow the step-by-step instructions on pages 24–41 and use the design on page 65.

2. Trace the leaf shapes (*fig. 1*) onto the *shiny* side of the iron-on Vilene.

3. Trace the rose shapes (*fig. 2*) onto the *shiny* side of the iron-on Vilene.

4. Refer to labels on the black-and-white design on page 65 for a guide to colours and stitches to use, and to the chart on page 21.

FIG. 1 LEAVES FOR HARMONY

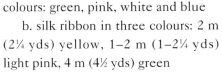

FIG. 2 ROSES FOR HARMONY

BORDEAUX

Materials

– IRON-ON VILENE OR FUSIBLE WEBBING: a strip of 10 cm (4 in)

– ROSES: two squares of light apricot fabric, each measuring 12 cm x 8 cm (5 in x 3¼ in); and one square of light dusty pink fabric measuring 7 cm x 7 cm (2¾ in x 2¾ in) for the roses (*see Which colours and textures do I use for fabric shapes?* on page 9)

– LEAVES: 20 cm x 9 cm (8 in x 3½ in) of green fabric (*see* page 9)

– BACKGROUND SQUARE: 50 cm x 50 cm (20 in x 20 in) of cream fabric (*see Which colours do I use for fabric backgrounds?* on page 41)

– BATTING/WADDING: a square measuring 55 cm x 55 cm (22 in x 22 in) (*see Which batting/wadding do I use?* on page 12)

– MUSLIN: a square measuring 55 cm x 55 cm (22 in x 22 in) (*see* page 12 if you will be framing the article)

– FOR EMBROIDERY: (*see Which threads and colours do I use?* on page 10)

a. two skeins of six-strand embroidery thread in dusty pink, one skein in darker rose pink and one in green

b. silk ribbon in the following three colours: 3 m (3¼ yds) light pink, 2 m (2¼ yds) apricot, 3 m (3¼ yds) green

– SATIN RIBBON ROSES: satin ribbon (*see* page 12 and the instructions on pages 22–24) in the following colours: 3 x 12 cm (5 in) dusty pink, 2 x 12 cm (5 in) apricot (i.e. a total of five lengths of ribbon)

– BEADS: one packet of pale green or cream beads, half a packet of cream teardrop beads and about ten larger pink beads (*see* page 11)

Method

1. Follow the step-by-step instructions on pages 24–41.
2. Trace the leaf shapes *(fig. 3)* onto the *shiny* side of the iron-on Vilene.
3. Trace the rose shapes *(fig. 4)* onto the *shiny* side of the iron-on Vilene.
4. Refer to the design on page 66 for a guide to colours and stitches to use, and to the chart on page 21.

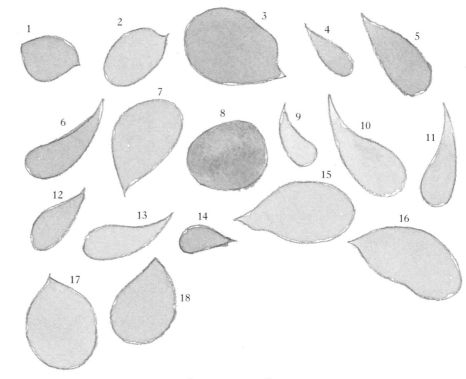

FIG. 3 LEAVES FOR BORDEAUX

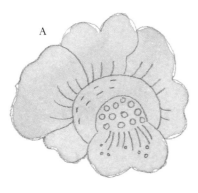
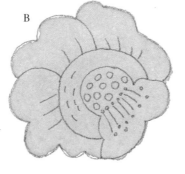
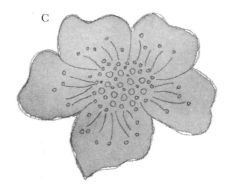

FIG. 4 ROSES FOR BORDEAUX

ANTOINETTE

Materials

– IRON-ON VILENE OR FUSIBLE WEBBING: a strip of 10 cm (4 in)

– ROSES: 15 cm x 10 cm (6 in x 4 in) light apricot fabric (*see Which colours and textures do I use for fabric shapes?* on page 9)

– BOW: 10 cm x 7 cm (4 in x 2¾ in) of darker apricot fabric (*see* page 9)

– LEAVES: 22 cm x 9 cm (9 in x 3½ in) of green fabric (*see* page 9)

– BACKGROUND SQUARE: 50 cm x 50 cm (20 in x 20 in) of cream fabric (*see Which colours do I use for fabric backgrounds?* on page 41)

– BATTING/WADDING: 55 cm x 55 cm (22 in x 22 in) (*see* page 12)

– MUSLIN: 55 cm x 55 cm (22 in x 22 in) (*see* page 12)

– FOR EMBROIDERY. (*see Which threads and colours do I use?* on page 10)

a. one skein of six-strand embroidery thread each of these colours: apricot, darker pink, green and blue

b. silk ribbon in these colours: 4 m (4¼ yds) light pink, 2–3 m (2¼–3¼ yds) apricot, 3 m (3¼ yds) yellow

– SATIN RIBBON ROSES: 5 x 12 cm (5 in) of dusty pink satin ribbon (*see* pages 12 and 22–24)

– BEADS: half a packet of cream beads and half a packet of darker or dusty pink beads for rose centres

Method

1. Follow the step-by-step instructions on pages 24–41.

2. Trace the 27 leaf shapes (*fig. 5*) onto the *shiny* side of the iron-on Vilene.

3. Trace the rose shapes and the bow (*fig. 6*) onto the *shiny* side of the iron-on Vilene. Draw one of each shape.

4. Refer to the labels on the black-and-white design on pages 67–68 for a guide to colours and stitches to use, and to the chart on page 21.

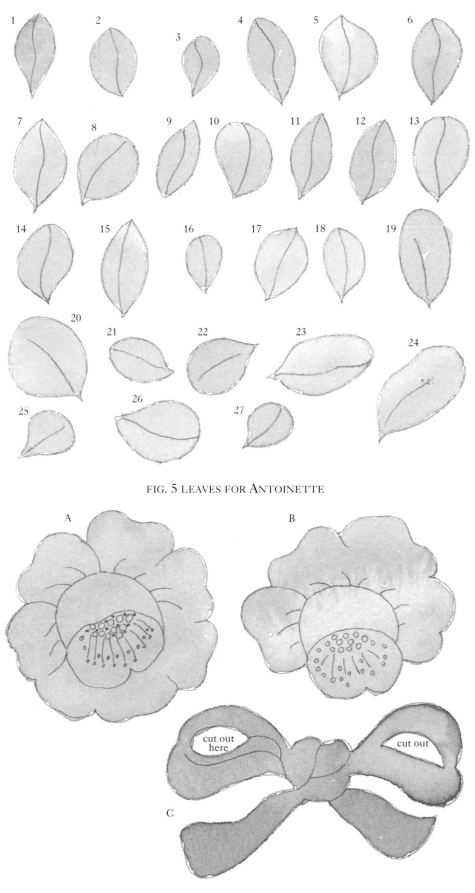

FIG. 5 LEAVES FOR ANTOINETTE

FIG. 6

RAPTURE

Materials

– IRON-ON VILENE OR FUSIBLE WEBBING: a strip of 10 cm (4 in)

– ROSES: 14 cm x 7 cm (5½ in x 2¾ in) of apricot fabric (*see Which colours and textures do I use for fabric shapes?* on page 9)

– LEAVES: 20 cm x 9 cm (8 in x 3½ in) of green fabric (*see* page 9)

– BACKGROUND SQUARE: 50 cm x 50 cm (20 in x 20 in) of cream fabric (*see* page 9)

– BATTING/WADDING: 55 cm x 55 cm (22 in x 22 in) (*see* page 9)

– MUSLIN: 55 cm x 55 cm (22 in x 22 in) (*see* page 12 if you will be framing the article)

– FOR EMBROIDERY: (*see Which threads and colours do I use?* on page 10)

a. one skein of six-strand embroidery thread in these colours: dusty pink, rose pink, green and blue

b. silk ribbon in three colours: 4 m (4½ yds) light pink, 3–4 m (3¼–4½ yds) apricot, 2 m (2 yds) yellow

– SATIN RIBBON ROSES: 6 x 12 cm (5 in) of dusty pink satin ribbon (*see* pages 12 and 22–24)

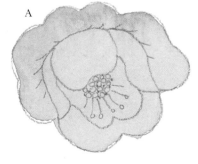

FIG. 8 ROSES FOR RAPTURE

– BEADS: half a packet of cream beads and half a packet of darker pink beads for rose centres (*see* page 11)

Method

1. Follow the step-by-step instructions on pages 24–41 and use the design on pages 69–70.
2. Trace the 25 leaf shapes (*fig. 7)* onto the *shiny* side of the iron-on Vilene. Draw one of each shape.
3. Trace the two rose shapes (*fig. 8)* onto the *shiny* side of the iron-on Vilene. Draw one of each shape.
4. Refer to the design on pages 69–70 for a guide to colours and stitches to use, and to the chart on page 21.

TRAVIATA

Materials

– IRON-ON VILENE OR FUSIBLE WEBBING: a strip of 10 cm (4 in) (see pages 14 and 28)

– ROSES: 20 cm x 10 cm (8 in x 4 in) of dusty pink fabric (*see* page 9)

– LEAVES: 20 cm x 10 cm (8 in x 4 in) of green fabric (*see* page 9)

– BACKGROUND SQUARE: 50 cm x 50 cm (20 in x 20 in) of cream fabric (*see* page 9)

– BATTING/WADDING: 55 cm x 55 cm (22 in x 22 in) (*see* page 12)

– MUSLIN: 55 cm x 55 cm (22 in x 22 in) (*see* page 12)

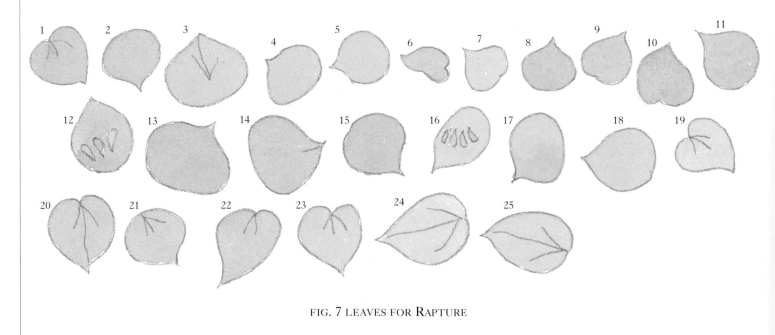

FIG. 7 LEAVES FOR RAPTURE

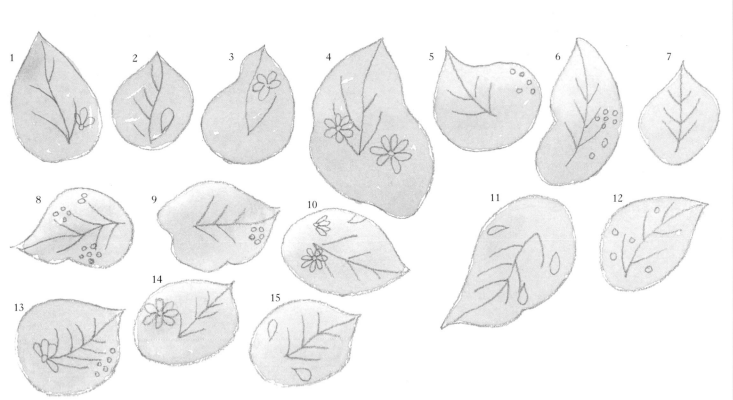

FIG. 9 LEAVES FOR TRAVIATA

– FOR EMBROIDERY: (*see Which threads and colours do I use?* on page 10)

a. one skein of six-strand embroidery thread each each of the following seven colours: dusty pink, rose pink, lilac, white, pale pink, green and blue

b. silk ribbon in six colours: 6 m (6½ yds) green, 3 m (3¼ yds) yellow, 3 m (3¼ yds) apricot, 2 m (2¼ yds) rose pink, 3 m (3¼ yds) pale pink, and 2 m (2¼ yds) aqua blue

– SATIN RIBBON ROSES: 8 x 12 cm (5 in) of dusty pink satin ribbon (*see* pages 12 and 22–24)

– BEADS: one packet of cream or green beads and half a packet of dusty pink beads for the centres of the roses (*see Why use beads?* on page 11)

Method

1. Follow the step-by-step instructions given on pages 24–41.
2. Trace the leaf shapes *(fig. 9)* onto the *shiny* side of the iron-on Vilene.
3. Trace the rose shapes *(fig. 10)* onto the *shiny* side of the iron-on Vilene.
4. Use the design on pages 70–71 and the chart on page 21 as a guide.

FIG. 10 ROSES FOR TRAVIATA

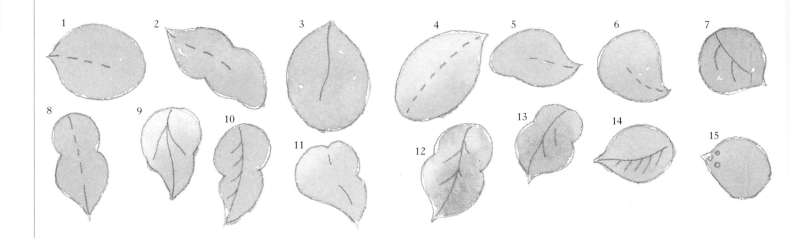

FIG. 11 LEAVES FOR SOLITAIRE

SOLITAIRE

Materials

– IRON-ON VILENE OR FUSIBLE WEBBING: a strip of 10 cm (4 in)

– FLOWERS: three squares of fabric, each in a different colour, and each measuring 7 cm x 7 cm (2¾ in x 2¾ in). The colours are blue, rust and red (*see* page 9).

– LEAVES: 20 cm x 9 cm (8 in x 3½ in) of green fabric (*see* page 9)

– BACKGROUND SQUARE: 50 cm x 50 cm (20 in x 20 in) of cream fabric (*see* page 9)

– BATTING/WADDING: 55 cm x 55 cm (22 in x 22 in) (*see* page 12)

– MUSLIN: 55 cm x 55 cm (22 in x 22 in) (*see* page 12 if you will be framing the article)

– FOR EMBROIDERY: (*see Which threads and colours do I use?* on page 10)

a. one skein of six-strand embroidery thread in green, blue and coral; and two skeins in red

b. silk ribbon in two colours: 4 m (4½ yds) dark cerise pink, 4–5 m (4½–5½ yds) teal blue

– SATIN RIBBON ROSES: 5 x 12 cm (5 in) of satin ribbon (*see* pages 12 and the instructions on pages 22–24)

– BEADS: one packet of green or red beads and two large teardrop-shaped beads for the top of the design

Method

1. Follow the step-by-step instructions on pages 24–41 and use the design on page 73.

2. Trace the 15 leaf shapes *(fig. 11)* onto the *shiny* side of the iron-on Vilene. Number the shapes on the *dull* side of the iron-on Vilene.

3. Trace the three flower shapes *(fig. 12)* onto the *shiny* side of the iron-on Vilene. (Make sure that you iron the correct shape onto the correct colour fabric – blue, red or rust.)

4. Refer to the labels on the black-and-white design supplied on page 73 for a guide to colours and stitches to use, and to the chart on page 21.

blue

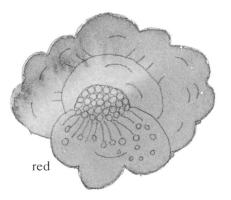

red

rust

FIG. 12 FLOWERS FOR SOLITAIRE

ROSE CHAIN

Materials

- IRON-ON VILENE OR FUSIBLE WEBBING: a strip of 15 cm (6 in)
- ROSES: 15 cm x 15 cm (6 in x 6 in) of pink fabric (*see Which colours and textures do I use for fabric shapes?* on page 9)
- LEAVES: a strip of 15 cm (6 in) of blue or green fabric (*see* page 9)
- BACKGROUND SQUARE: 57 cm x 57 cm (22½ in x 22½ in) of cream fabric for a square without borders (*see Which colours do I use for fabric backgrounds?* on page 9) OR

42 cm x 42 cm (16½ in x 16½ in) of cream fabric for a cushion square with a border (*see* step 9, *Attach the border strips*, on page 32)
- BATTING/WADDING: 57 cm x 57 cm (22½ in x 22½ in) (*see* page 9)
- MUSLIN: 57 cm x 57 cm (22½ in x 22½ in) (*see* page 12 if you will be framing the article)
- FOR EMBROIDERY: (*see Which threads and colours do I use?* on page 10)

a. one skein of six-strand embroidery thread in each of the following six colours: light pink, medium pink, darker pink, blue, green and cream (for quilting the central blocks)

b. 3 m (3¼ yds) of green silk ribbon
- SATIN RIBBON ROSES: 20 x 12 cm (5 in) of pink satin ribbon (*see* page 12 and the instructions on pages 22–24)
- BEADS: one packet of small blue, pink or green seed beads for the rose centres and corners of the design
- BORDERS (optional): 57 cm x 25 cm (22½ in x 10 in) of fabric in pink, blue or green to complement the design (*see* page 32)

Method

1. Follow the step-by-step instructions given on pages 24–41 and use the design on page 74.

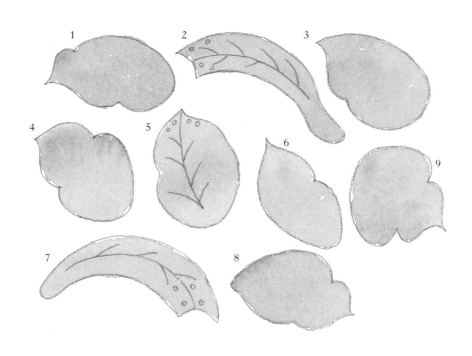

FIG. 13 SHAPES FOR ROSE CHAIN

2. Draw two of each shape (*fig. 13*) onto the *shiny* side of the iron-on Vilene, and two of each shape onto the *dull* side. Iron onto blue fabric.
3. Draw two of the rose shapes (*fig. 14*) on the *shiny* side of the Vilene and two on the *dull* side. Iron onto pink fabric.
4. Refer to the labels on the black-and-white design on page 74 for a guide to colours and stitches to use, and to the chart on page 21.

FIG. 14 ROSE FOR ROSE CHAIN

ODYSSEY

Materials

- IRON-ON VILENE OR FUSIBLE WEBBING: a strip of 15 cm (6 in)
- FLOWERS A AND B: 15 cm x 30 cm (6 in x 12 in) of light pink fabric (*see Which colours and textures do I use for fabric shapes?* on page 9)
- FLOWER C: 15 cm x 15 cm (6 in x 6 in) of darker pink fabric (*see* page 9)
- FOUR MOON-SHAPED WREATHS: 25 cm x 25 cm (10 in x 10 in) of light green fabric (*see* page 9)
- LEAVES: 10 cm x 10 cm (4 in x 4 in) of darker green fabric (*see* page 9)

BACKGROUND SQUARE: 57 cm x 57 cm (22½ in x 22½ in) of cream fabric (for a square without a border) OR

42 cm x 42 cm (16½ in x 16½ in) of cream fabric (for a square with a border)

BATTING/WADDING: 57 cm x 57 cm (22½ in x 22½ in) (*see Which batting/wadding do I use?* on page 12)

FOR EMBROIDERY (*see Which threads and colours do I use?* on page 10):

FIG. 15 leaf for Odyssey

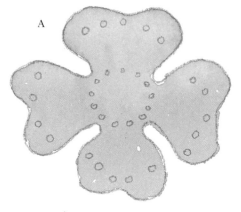

A

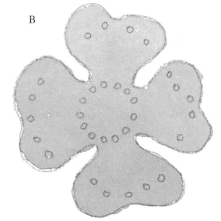

B

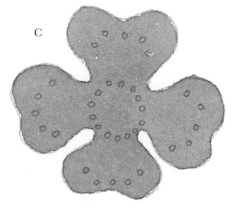

C

FIG. 16 flowers for Odyssey

a. one skein of six-strand embroidery thread in each of the following five colours: dusty pink, lighter green, darker green, blue and darker blue (for couching)

b. silk ribbon: 5–6 m (5½–6½ yds) blue, 8–9 m (8¾–9¾ yds) yellow, 2 m (2¼ yds) rose pink

– Satin ribbon roses: satin ribbon (*see* pages 12 and 22–24) in two colours: 8 x 12 cm (6 in) in dusty pink and 8 x 12 cm (6 in) in lighter pink (i.e. 16 lengths of ribbon in total)

– Borders (optional): 57 cm x 25 cm (22½ in x 10 in) of fabric in a colour that complements the design: pink, blue or green (*see* step 9, *Attach the border strips*, on page 32)

Method

1. Follow the step-by-step instructions on pages 24–41 and use the design on page 75.
2. Draw two leaf shapes *(fig. 15)* onto the *shiny* side of the Vilene, and two shapes onto the *dull* side of the Vilene.
3. Draw two of each flower *(fig. 16)* onto the *shiny* side of the Vilene, and two of each flower onto the *dull* side.
4. Draw two moon shapes *(fig. 17)* onto *each* side of the Vilene as well.
5. Refer to the design on page 75 for a guide to colours and stitches to use, and to the chart on page 21.

FIG. 17 moon shape for Odyssey

MONARCH

Materials

– IRON-ON VILENE OR FUSIBLE WEBBING: a strip of 10 cm (4 in)

– ROSE PETALS A AND B: 20 cm x 6 cm (8 in x 2¼ in) of pink fabric (see Which colours and textures do I use for fabric shapes? on page 9)

– LEAF C: 12 cm x 6 cm (5 in x 2¼ in) of green fabric (see page 9)

– BACKGROUND SQUARE: 57 cm x 57 cm (22½ in x 22½ in) of cream fabric for a square without borders OR 42 cm x 42 cm (16½ in x 16½ in) of cream fabric for a square with a border (see page 14)

– BATTING/WADDING: 57 cm x 57 cm (22½ in x 22½ in) (see page 12)

– MUSLIN: 57 cm x 57 cm (22½ in x 22½ in) (see page 12)

– FOR EMBROIDERY: (see Which threads and colours do I use? on page 10)

a. two skeins of six-strand embroidery thread in darker green and rose pink; one skein each in lighter green, dusty pink, lilac and yellow

b. silk ribbon in the following three colours: 13–15 m (14¼–16½ yds) darker green, 4–5 m (4¼–5½ yds) dusty pink (for the outer square) and 4–5 m (4¼–5½ yds) rose pink (for around the rose petals)

– SATIN RIBBON ROSES: 16 x 12 cm (5 in) rose pink satin ribbon (see pages 12 and 22–24)

– BEADS: one packet of larger pink beads for the central squares, and one packet of smaller green beads for below the fabric leaves (see page 11)

Method

1. Follow the step-by-step instructions on pages 24–41 and use the design on page 76.

2. Draw four A petals (fig. 18) on the shiny side of the iron-on Vilene/fusible webbing and four A petals onto the dull side of the iron-on Vilene.

3. Draw two B petals (fig. 18) onto the shiny side of the Vilene and two B petals onto the dull side of the Vilene.

4. Draw four leaf C shapes (fig. 18) onto the shiny side of the Vilene and four leaf C shapes onto the dull side.

5. Refer to the design on page 76 for a guide to colours and stitches to use, and to the chart on page 21.

NOTE

Thread the 4–5 m (4¼–5½ yds) of dusty pink silk ribbon and bring the needle up from the back of the work to run the ribbon between two rows of green couching sewn to form the squares. Insert the needle and bring it from the back to the front again each time to start and end off the squares. Stitch this ribbon down on the background fabric by quilting along the centre of the ribbon or along the edges, using two strands of matching dusty pink embroidery thread.

RIBBONS AND BOWS

Materials

– IRON-ON VILENE OR FUSIBLE WEBBING: a strip of 15 cm (6 in)

– ROSES 1 AND 2 (fig. 20): 14 cm x 28 cm (5½ in x 11 in) of dusty pink fabric (see Which colours and textures do I use for fabric shapes? on page 9)

– FLOWERS 1,2, 3 (fig. 21) AND CENTRAL FLOWER (fig. 22): 12 cm x 25 cm (5 in x 10 in) lighter pink fabric

– ROSE LEAVES 1–6 (fig. 19): 30 cm x 10 cm (12 in x 4 in) darker green fabric (see page 9)

– FLOWER LEAVES 7–10 (fig. 19) AND LEAF A (fig. 23) : 15 cm x 25 cm (6 in x 10 in) of lighter green fabric

– BACKGROUND SQUARE: 57 cm x 57 cm (22½ in x 22½ in) of cream or pale oyster pink fabric for a square without borders (see page 41) OR 42 cm x 42 cm (16½ in x 16½ in) of cream or pale oyster pink fabric for a square with a border

– BORDERS (optional): 57 cm x 25 cm (22½ in x 10 in) of fabric (see page 32) in a green or dusty pink colour

– BATTING/WADDING: 57 cm x 57 cm (22½ in x 22½ in) (see page 12)

– MUSLIN: 57 cm x 57 cm (22½ in x 22½ in) (see page 12)

– FOR EMBROIDERY: (see Which threads and colours do I use? on page 10)

a. two to three skeins of six-strand embroidery thread in lighter green, two skeins in rose pink, and one skein each in dusty pink, darker green and light pink

b. silk ribbon: 5 m (5½ yds) rose pink and 8 m (8¾ yds) light green

c. embroidery thread in shades matching the fabric shapes (for edges)

– SATIN RIBBON ROSES: 24 x 12 cm (5 in) of dusty pink satin ribbon (see pages 12 and 22–24)

– BEADS: one packet of green or dusty pink beads

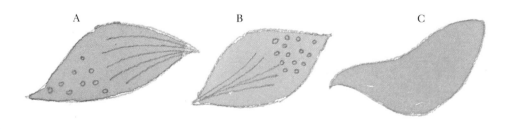

FIG. 5 PETAL AND LEAF SHAPES FOR MONARCH

Method

1. Follow the step-by-step instructions on pages 24–41 and use the design on page 77.

2. Draw one central flower *(fig. 22)* onto the *shiny* side of the iron-on Vilene. Iron onto lighter pink fabric.

3. Draw one shape A leaf *(fig. 23)* onto the the *shiny* side of the iron-on Vilene and one shape A leaf onto the *dull* side. Iron onto lighter green fabric.

4. Draw all the other shapes *twice* onto the *shiny* side of the iron-on Vilene and *twice* onto the *dull* side.

5. Clearly label (with numbers or letters) all the roses, flowers and leaves on the *dull* side of the Vilene.

6. Refer to the labels on the black-and-white design on page 77 for a guide to colours and stitches to use, and to the chart on page 21.

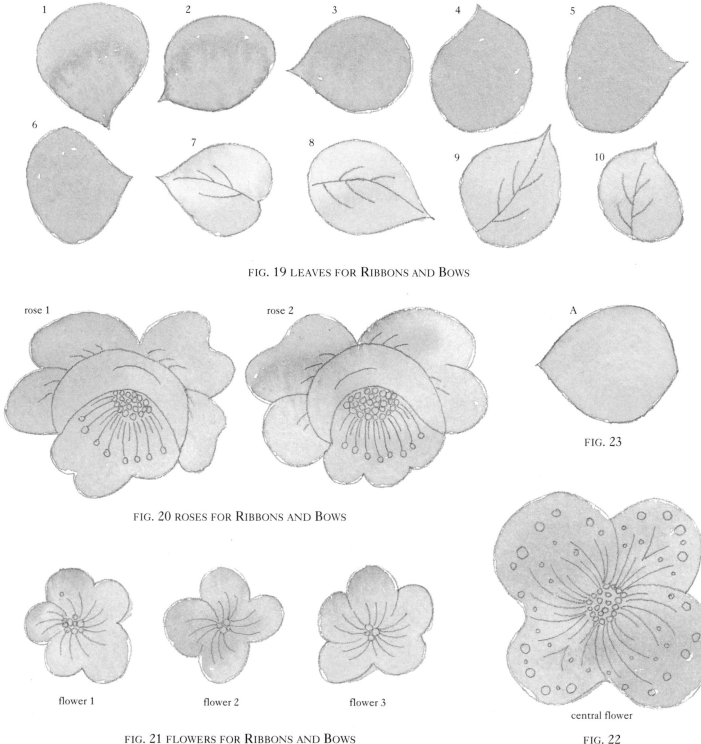

FIG. 19 LEAVES FOR RIBBONS AND BOWS

FIG. 20 ROSES FOR RIBBONS AND BOWS

FIG. 23

FIG. 21 FLOWERS FOR RIBBONS AND BOWS

FIG. 22

Camrose

Materials

- IRON-ON VILENE OR FUSIBLE WEBBING: a strip of 15 cm (6 in)
- ROSES: 40 cm x 10 cm (16 in x 4 in) of apricot fabric (*see Which colours and textures do I use for fabric shapes?* on page 9).
- SMALLER FLOWERS A, B AND C (*fig. 26*): 21 cm x 10 cm (8¼ in x 4 in) of dusty pink fabric (*see* page 9)
- LEAVES: 15 cm x 42 cm (6 in x 16½ in) of green fabric (*see* page 9)
- BACKGROUND SQUARE: 57 cm x 57 cm (22½ in x 22½ in) of cream fabric for a square without borders (*see Which colours do I use for fabric backgrounds?* on page 9) OR

42 cm x 42 cm (16½ in x 16½ in) of cream fabric for a square with a border (*see* page 32)
- BATTING/WADDING: 57 cm x 57 cm (22½ in x 22½ in) (*see* page 12)
- MUSLIN: 57 cm x 57 cm (22½ in x 22½ in) (*see* page 12 if you will be framing the article)
- FOR EMBROIDERY: (*see Which threads and colours do I use?* on page 10)

a. two skeins of six-strand embroidery thread each in dusty pink and green; one skein each in rose pink, apricot and cream (for the quilted central blocks)

b. about 5–6 m (5½–6½ yds) of green silk ribbon
- SATIN RIBBON ROSES: satin ribbon (*see* pages 12 and 22–24) in two colours: 20 x 12 cm (5 in) in lighter apricot, and 10 x 12 cm (5 in) in lighter pink (i.e. 30 lengths of ribbon in total)
- BEADS: one packet of light green or dusty pink or cream beads, and half a packet of cream teardrop beads
- BORDERS (optional): 57 cm x 25 cm (22½ in x 10 in) of fabric in peach or green (*see* step 9, *Attach the border strips*, on page 32)

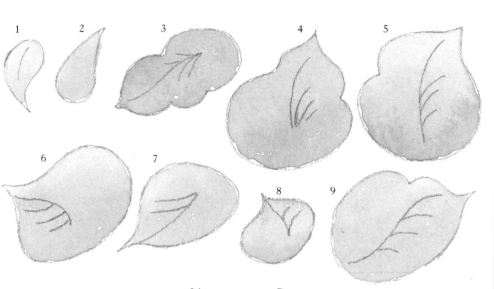

FIG. 24 LEAVES FOR CAMROSE

FIG. 25 ROSE FOR CAMROSE

Method

1. Follow the step-by-step instructions on pages 24–41.
2. Draw two of each leaf shape (*fig. 24*) onto the *shiny* side of the Vilene and two of each leaf onto the *dull* side.
3. Draw two of the rose shape (*fig. 25*) and two of each flower shape (*fig. 26*) onto the *shiny* side of the Vilene and two of each onto the *dull* side.
4. Refer to the design on page 78, and to the chart on page 21.

A

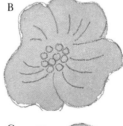

B

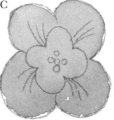

C

FIG. 26

FILIGREE

Materials

– IRON-ON VILENE OR FUSIBLE WEBBING: a strip of 10 cm (4 in) (*see* pages 14 and 28)

– ROSES: one square of blue fabric measuring 10 cm x 10 cm (4 in x 4 in), and one square of dusty pink fabric, also measuring 10 cm x 10 cm (4 in x 4 in) (*see Which colours and textures do I use for fabric shapes?* on page 9)

– LEAVES: 10 cm x 10 cm (4 in x 4 in) of green fabric (*see* page 9)

– BACKGROUND SQUARE: 50 cm x 50 cm (20 in x 20 in) of cream or off-white fabric (*see Which colours do I use for fabric backgrounds?* on page 41)

– BATTING/WADDING: 55 cm x 55 cm (22 in x 22 in) (*see* page 12)

– MUSLIN: 55 cm x 55 cm (22 in x 22 in) (*see* page 12 if framing the design)

– FOR EMBROIDERY: (*see Which threads and colours do I use?* on page 10)

a. two skeins of good quality six-strand embroidery thread each in dusty pink and green; one skein of embroidery thread each in blue, yellow and lavender

b. Silk ribbon in the following eight colours:

❖ 2–3 m (2¼–3¼ yds) light green
❖ 1 m (1 yd) dark lavender/grape.
❖ 2 m (2¼ yds) dusty pink
❖ 2 m (2¼ yds) teal blue
❖ 1 m (1 yd) rose pink
❖ 2 m (2¼ yds) light pink
❖ 1 m (1 yd) aqua green
❖ 1 m (1 yd) lavender

– BEADS: one packet of blue seed beads, and half a packet of plum or pink seed beads (*see Why use beads?* on page 11).

– No satin ribbon roses are used

Method

1. Follow the step-by-step instructions on pages 24–41 and use the design on pages 79–80.
2. Trace one of each leaf shape (*fig.27*) onto the *shiny* side of the Vilene. Number each shape on the *dull* side.
3. Trace one of each rose shape (*fig. 28*) onto the *shiny* side of the Vilene.
4. Refer to the design on pages 79–80 for a guide to colours and stitches to use, and to the chart on page 21.

SIX-BLOCK BABY'S QUILT

Materials

Although the *Tegan-L, Dale-L, Sarah-Lee, Lauren-Jane, Jason-V* and *Guylin-V* designs are used for making up the *Six-block baby's quilt*, these designs are equally suitable for making smaller cushions (you can add borders) or quilt squares. The chapter called *Other projects* will give you a list of materials to purchase for the squares using these designs (pages 60–61), and explain how to make up this beautiful cot quilt (page 61).

Method for all six designs

1. Follow the step-by-step instructions on pages 24–41 and refer to the relevant designs on pages 85–90.
2. Trace the shapes for the relevant designs on pages 55–57.
3. Trace the leaf shapes for the lighter green fabric onto the iron-on Vilene as instructed at each design.
4. Trace the leaf shapes for the darker green fabric onto the iron-on Vilene as instructed at each design.
5. Trace the rose shapes for the darker apricot fabric onto the iron-on Vilene as instructed at each design.
6. Refer to the labels on the black-and-white designs on pages 85–90 for a guide to colours and stitches to use, and to the chart on page 21.

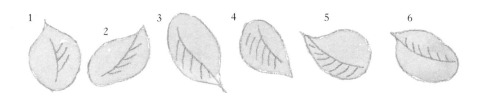

FIG. 27 LEAVES FOR FILIGREE

FIG. 28 ROSES FOR FILIGREE

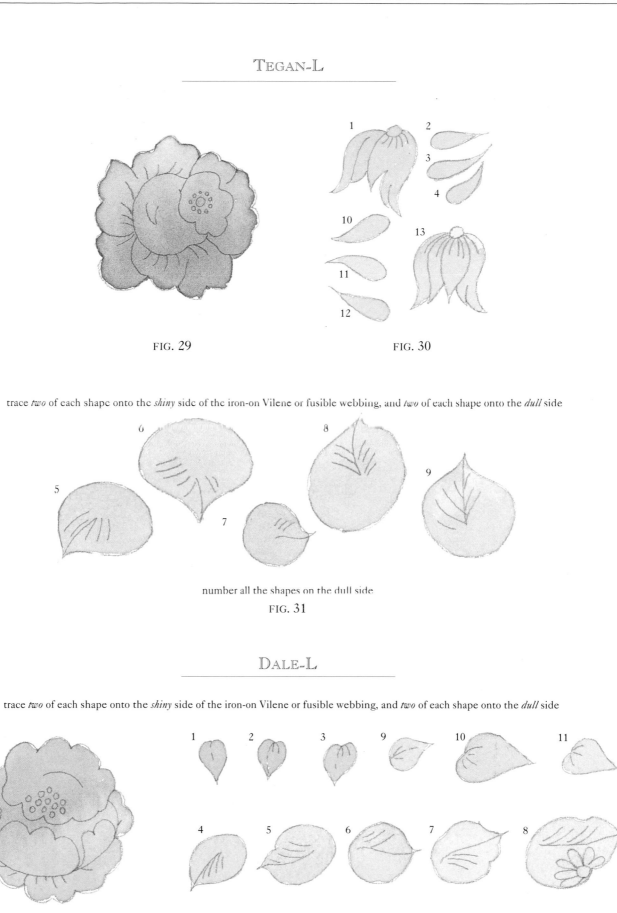

TEGAN-L

FIG. 29   FIG. 30

trace *two* of each shape onto the *shiny* side of the iron-on Vilene or fusible webbing, and *two* of each shape onto the *dull* side

number all the shapes on the dull side

FIG. 31

DALE-L

trace *two* of each shape onto the *shiny* side of the iron-on Vilene or fusible webbing, and *two* of each shape onto the *dull* side

number all the shapes on the dull side

FIG. 32

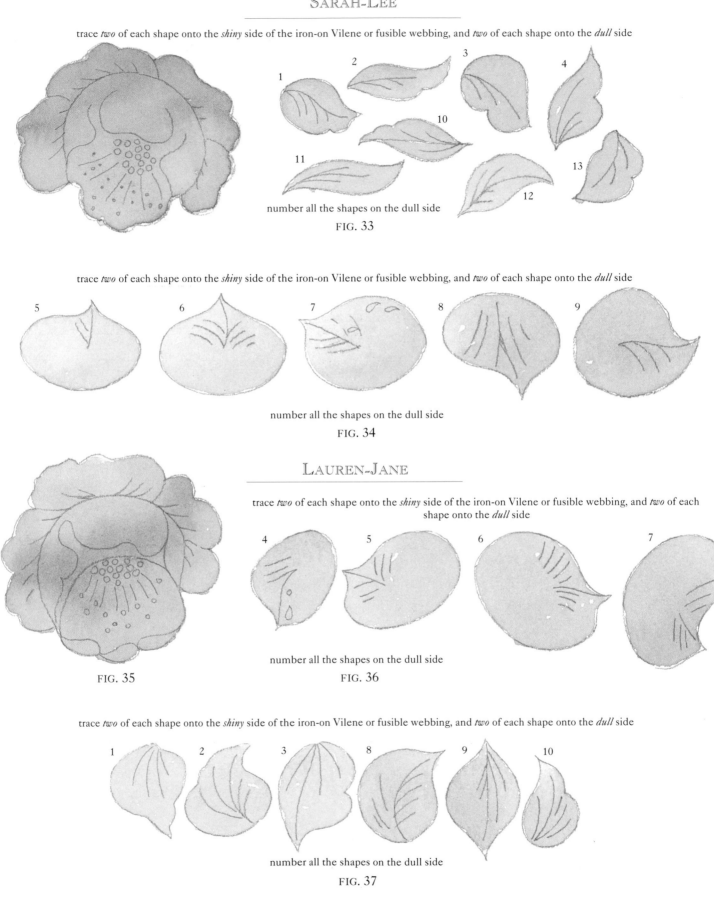

SARAH-LEE

trace *two* of each shape onto the *shiny* side of the iron-on Vilene or fusible webbing, and *two* of each shape onto the *dull* side

number all the shapes on the dull side

FIG. 33

trace *two* of each shape onto the *shiny* side of the iron-on Vilene or fusible webbing, and *two* of each shape onto the *dull* side

number all the shapes on the dull side

FIG. 34

LAUREN-JANE

trace *two* of each shape onto the *shiny* side of the iron-on Vilene or fusible webbing, and *two* of each shape onto the *dull* side

FIG. 35

number all the shapes on the dull side

FIG. 36

trace *two* of each shape onto the *shiny* side of the iron-on Vilene or fusible webbing, and *two* of each shape onto the *dull* side

number all the shapes on the dull side

FIG. 37

JASON-V

trace *two* of each shape onto the *shiny* side of the iron-on Vilene or fusible webbing, and *two* of each shape onto the *dull* side

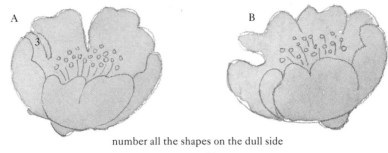

number all the shapes on the dull side

FIG. 38

trace *two* of each shape onto the *shiny* side of the iron-on Vilene or fusible webbing, and *two* of each shape onto the *dull* side

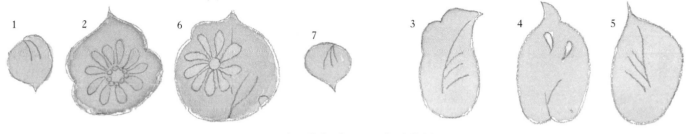

number all the shapes on the dull side

FIG. 39

GUYLIN-V

trace *two* of each shape onto the *shiny* side of the iron on Vilene or fusible webbing, and *two* of each shape onto the *dull* side

number all the shapes on the dull side

FIG. 40

trace *two* of each shape onto the *shiny* side of the iron-on Vilene or fusible webbing, and *two* of each shape onto the *dull* side

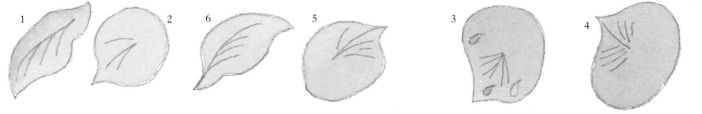

number all the shapes on the dull side

FIG. 41

OTHER PROJECTS

This chapter contains instructions for making a variety of projects, each using ribbon embroidery as a decorative feature. The *Four-block quilt* and *Baby's quilt*, which are both less daunting to the inexperienced needleworker than a full-size quilt, make wonderful gifts for new mothers and may well become precious heirlooms. The bridesmaid's dress is simple enough for anyone to make, yet looks quite spectacular. Add satin ballet shoes decorated with ribbon roses and an Alice band to the dress and you have an outfit fit for a princess. The porcelain doll also makes a wonderful gift for someone special.

FOUR-BLOCK QUILT

This makes a lovely wall quilt for an entrance hall, passage or bedroom (*see the photograph at the beginning of the book*). It can also be used as a beautiful sofa throw. The *Victorian Trellis, Acanthus, Byzantine* and *Pompeii* designs were used for this quilt. To make up a larger quilt for the bedroom, make 12 or 16 squares.

Materials

The materials listed below are for making one square. Multiply the material requirements by the number of squares you need. The requirements for the embroidery threads and silk ribbon are only a rough guideline, as your choice of stitches will ultimately determine how much you need of each.

– IRON-ON VILENE/FUSIBLE WEBBING: a strip measuring 25–50 cm (10–20 in) (*see pages 14 and 28*)

– FLOWERS AND LEAVES AND OTHER FABRIC SHAPES: Use strips of fabric, each measuring about 15 cm (6 in), in polysilk, cotton, chintz or pure silk. You will need one strip in each of the following colours to make the fabric shapes:

  a. lighter dusty pink or plum
  b. dusty pink
  c. peppermint green or pale jade
  d. lighter apricot or peach

  e. darker apricot or peach
  f. blue
  g. lavender.

– BACKGROUND SQUARE: 57 cm x 57 cm (22½ in x 22½ in) of pure silk, polysilk, cotton or chintz fabric in cream, pale oyster (pink), green or peach for making a quilt square without borders. Draw a smaller square measuring 50 cm x 50 cm (20 in x 20 in) inside the outer square.

– BATTING/WADDING: 57 cm x 57 cm (22½ in x 22½ in) (*see Which batting/ wadding do I use?* on page 12)

– MUSLIN: 57 cm x 57 cm (22½ in x 22½ in) (*see page 12*)

– BACKING FABRIC: Refer to *Which fabric is best for backing cushions and quilts?* (page 12) and to *Attaching the backing* (page 39)

– FOR EMBROIDERY (*see Which threads and colours do I use?* on page 10):

  a. two skeins of six-strand embroidery thread in green, blue and lighter apricot or peach; one skein each in light dusty pink or plum, dusty pink, darker apricot and lavender

  b. silk ribbon in each of the following three colours:
❖ 5–10 m (5½–11 yds) light green
❖ 4–8 m (4½–8¾ yds) light blue
❖ 5–10 m (5½–11 yds) light pink

– BEADS: 4–8 large, round, dusty pink beads, and a quarter of a packet of smaller green beads (or any other complementary colour)

– QUILT FINISH:

  a. You will need four strips of binding fabric, each measuring 6 cm (2¼ in) in width. Each strip is cut as long as the longest side of the quilt. Use a complementary shade of blue, salmon or green fabric.

  b. If you are making a wall quilt, you will also need extra fabric for making loops for it to hang from. I suggest the same fabric as the borders.

Method

1. Follow the step-by-step instructions on pages 24–41 and use the designs on pages 81, 82, 83 and 84. Owing to limited space in the chapter on *Design Details*, no individual shapes for these designs have been supplied. Working directly from the joined designs, trace each individual shape onto the *shiny* side of the iron-on Vilene/fusible webbing. Number each shape on the *dull* side. Iron the Vilene/webbing shapes onto the relevant colour fabric as indicated on the design.

Join the squares and make up the quilt

1. Remove each square from the quilting hoop when you have completed the work, and embroider any remaining detail at the corners by hand without using the hoop.

2. Prepare each square as you would in the case of a cushion or quilt

HERE THE TEGAN-L DESIGN FROM THE BABY'S QUILT IS COMBINED WITH RIBBON EMBROIDERY (LEFT) AND CANDLEWICKING (RIGHT)

(*see* page 36). Zigzag all along the pencilled line and cut off the excess fabric and batting along the stitched edge. A square measuring 50 cm x 50 cm (20 in x 20 in) is ready to be joined to other squares.

3. Following the instructions given on page 38, join the squares.

4. Attach the backing to the joined squares, following the instructions given on page 39.

5. Attach the decorative cord or lace (optional) following the instructions given on pages 39–40.

6. Finish the quilt with binding following the instructions given on pages 40–41.

NOTE
Add loops if necessary to suspend the quilt from a rod against a wall.

SIX-BLOCK BABY'S QUILT

The baby's quilt uses the following six designs: *Tegan-L*, *Dale-L*, *Sarah-Lee*, *Lauren-Jane*, *Jason-V* and *Guylin-V*. Each of these designs measures 30 cm x 30 cm (12 in x 12 in) and is equally suitable for making a small cushion rather than a quilt square.

If you would like to use these designs to make up a large quilt, you will need to make more squares than you would if you were using the larger designs such as *Rose Chain* or *Pompeii*.

Materials
The materials listed below are for making one square of the quilt. Multiply the material requirements by the number of squares you need (I have used six). The requirements for the embroidery threads and silk ribbon are only a rough guideline, as your particular choice of stitches will ultimately determine how much you need of each of these.

– IRON-ON VILENE/FUSIBLE WEBBING: a strip measuring 15 cm (6 in) in width (*see* pages 14 and 28)

– ROSES: Use polysilk, chintz, cotton or polycotton fabric (*see Which colours and textures do I use for fabric shapes?* on page 9). You will need a strip of darker apricot fabric measuring 10 cm (4 in) in width.

– LEAVES: Use polysilk, chintz, cotton or polycotton fabric (*see Which colours and textures do I use for fabric shapes?* on page 9). You will need a strip of darker green fabric measuring 10 cm (4 in) in width, and an identical strip in lighter green.

– BACKGROUND SQUARE: Use poly-silk or cotton fabric in cream, or in a pale shade of apricot, pink or green. You will require 156 cm (1¾ yds) of fabric for six squares. Cut each square to measure 52 cm x 52 cm (20½ in x 20½ in) (for a square without borders). Draw a square measuring 32 cm x 32 cm (12½ in x 12½ in) inside the larger square to indicate the final cutting line (when completed).

NOTE

For those of you wishing to make a larger quilt, draw a larger square of up to about 40 cm x 40 cm (15¾ in x 15¾ in) (see Cut out the background fabric square *on page 29 in the chapter called* Step-by-step instructions*).*

– BACKING FABRIC: Refer to *Which fabric is best for backing cushions and quilts?* (page 12) and *Attaching the backing* (page 39).

– BATTING/WADDING: 52 cm x 52 cm (20½ in x 20½ in) (*see Which batting/wadding do I use?* on page 12)

– MUSLIN: 52 cm x 52 cm (20½ in x 20½ in) for backing

– FOR EMBROIDERY (*see Which threads and colours do I use?* on page 10):

a. one or two skeins of six-strand embroidery thread in green; one skein each in peach/apricot, light pink and rose pink thread

b. silk ribbon in these colours:

❖ 3–6 m (3¼–6½ yds) light pink

❖ 3–6 m (3¼–6½ yds) light green

– BEADS: an eighth of a packet of small seed beads in green or apricot

– QUILT FINISH:

a. You need four strips of binding, each measuring 6 cm (2¼ in) in width. Each strip is cut as long as the longest side of the quilt. Use a complementary shade of green or peach fabric.

b. decorative cord or lace (this is optional) (*see* pages 39–40)

– a quilting hoop with a diameter of 41 cm (16 in) (*see* page 13)

– Also refer to *Which other materials or equipment do I need?* on page 14

Method

Each of the six designs uses the same fabrics, colours, stitches and threads. Refer to the designs on pages 85–90 for a guide to colours and stitches to use, and to the chart on page 21.

1. Follow the step-by-step instructions on pages 24–41.

2. Refer to the section on the *Six-block baby's quilt* on page 54 when tracing onto the Vilene/fusible webbing.

3. Cut out the background fabric following the instructions on page 29, and draw a square of 32 cm x 32 cm (12½ in x 12½ in) inside the larger square. Pin the design to the background fabric following the instructions given on page 30.

4. Glue and position all the fabric shapes onto the background fabric following the instructions on page 31.

5. Trace the remaining detail of the design onto the background square following the instructions on page 31.

6. Place the layers in the quilting hoop following the instructions given on pages 32–33.

7. Embroider the six designs following the instructions given on the individual designs (pages 85–90) and by referring to the chart on page 21.

Join the squares and make up the quilt

Please use the same instructions for joining and making up that were given for the *Four-block quilt* on page 59, following steps 2–7. In step 2, however, each square for the *Six-block baby's quilt* will measure 32 cm x 32 cm (12½ in x 12½ in).

TRAVIATA IS USED FOR THIS FRAMED PICTURE, AND RIBBONS AND BOWS FOR THE CUSHION

HERE AN ALICE BAND WITH RIBBON ROSES COMPLEMENTS THE PRINCESS DESIGN

BRIDESMAID'S DRESS

This is a simple but really exciting project for a wedding or special occasion. Use a dress pattern that will give you an opportunity to embroider either a collar or a bodice. I used the *Princess* design (*see* pages 62–64 and page 91) to illustrate the technique.

HINT
If you find the Princess *design too long for the collar or bodice of your particular dress pattern, leave out leaf shapes number 1, 2, 3, 14, 15, and 16.*

Dress materials
Refer to the manufacturer's instructions on the dress pattern to find out how much fabric to buy before following the method outlined below. Also refer to the *Material requirements* on

page 5. You may have to adjust the requirements mentioned here to suit your particular pattern.

NOTES
❖ *I made this very special little dress using 100% silk fabric, but taffetta, polysilk, shantung, glazed cotton or 100% cotton fabrics are also quite suitable for this purpose.*

❖ *You will need to buy about ½–1 m (½–1 yd) of additional dress fabric to accommodate the embroidered collar or bodice, as they are positioned centrally on a square* (fig. 1). *This allows the design that is to be embroidered to fit well in a quilting hoop with a diameter of 35.5 cm (14 in) or 46 cm (18 in) (see* Which quilting hoop do I use and why? *on page 13, and step 6,* Pin the design to the background fabric square *on page 30).*

– 3–5 m (3¼–5½ yds) of dress fabric, the exact amount depending on the age of the child and the dress pattern you have chosen

– 50 cm (½ yd) of contrast fabric to make binding for the collar, sleeves and/or skirt of the dress (or you can buy ready-made binding)

– suitable fabric for lining the dress, according to the pattern manufacturer's instructions

– any other requirements listed on the dress pattern, e.g. interfacing, a zip, hooks and eyes, lace, etc.

Embroidery materials
– IRON-ON VILENE/FUSIBLE WEBBING: a strip measuring 10 cm (4 in) in width (*see* pages 14 and 28)

– BACKGROUND SQUARE: 50–57 cm x 50–57 cm (20–22½ in x 20–22½ in) of your chosen dress fabric

– BATTING/WADDING: a square of very thin batting/wadding, measuring the same size as the square of dress fabric above, to be used as a backing square for the collar or bodice

– MUSLIN: a square, measuring the same size as the above squares, to back the batting/wadding

– BACKING: a square of lining fabric, measuring the same size as the above squares, to back the embroidered panel once it has been completed

shape of collar

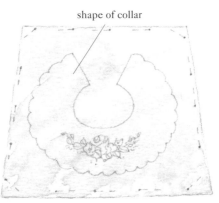

pin traced design onto background fabric

FIG. 1

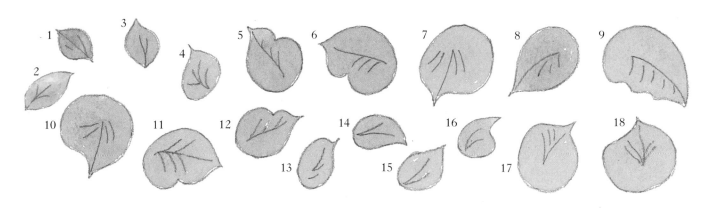

FIG. 2 LEAVES FOR PRINCESS DESIGN

– ROSES: two squares of lighter pink fabric, each measuring 10 cm x 10 cm (4 in x 4 in), and one square of darker pink fabric measuring 10 cm x 10 cm (4 in x 4 in) (*see Which other materials or equipment do I need?* on page 14, and *Which colours and textures do I use for fabric shapes?* on page 9)

– LEAVES: 15 cm x 15 cm (6 in x 6 in) of green fabric (*see Which colours and textures do I use for fabric shapes?* on page 9)

– FOR EMBROIDERY: (*see Which threads and colours do I use?* on page 10)

a. one skein of six-strand embroidery thread in each of the following colours: green, rose pink, dusty pink, lavender and yellow

b. silk ribbon in each of the following complementary colours:
❖ 3–4 m (3¼–4½ yds) green
❖ 3–4 m (3¼–4½ yds) light pink
❖ 2–3 m (2¼–3¼ yds) light blue

– SATIN RIBBON ROSES: 3 x 12 cm (6 in) dusty pink satin ribbon, and 4 x 12 cm (6 in) light pink satin ribbon (i.e. seven lengths in total) to make the roses (*see pages 12 and 22–24*)

– BEADS: half a packet of small light blue, dusty pink or green beads

– the necessary sewing aids (*see Which other materials or equipment do I need?* on page 14), including a quilting hoop with a diameter of either 35.5 cm (14 in) or 46 cm (18 in), depending on the size of the collar or bodice you have chosen to embroider

Method

1. Follow the step-by-step instructions on pages 24–41, referring to the *Princess* design on page 91 and to the shapes given on this page.

2. Using your chosen dress pattern, draw the outline of the collar or bodice onto the background square (*see* fig. 1 on the previous page).

3. Trace all the shapes for the *Princess* design onto the *shiny* side of the iron-on Vilene/fusible webbing. Number all the shapes on the *dull* side. Iron each shape onto fabric of the relevant colour.

4. Carefully glue and position the fabric shapes onto the background fabric using the instructions given on page 29.

A

C

B

FIG. 2 ROSES FOR PRINCESS DESIGN

tack bodice or collar to backing fabric
then cut off excess fabric, batting/wadding,
muslin and lining/backing

FIG. 4 TO LEAVE A SEAM ALLOWANCE

5. Trace the remaining detail onto the background square following the instructions given on page 31.

6. Place all the layers of fabric into a quilting hoop following the instructions given on pages 32–33.

7. Embroider the design following the instructions on the design (page 91), and refer to the chart on page 21.

8. Once all the embroidery work has been completed, pin the lining (backing) fabric to the embroidered square, wrong sides together.

9. Tack the collar or bodice to the backing fabric along the pencilled outline and cut off the excess fabric, batting/wadding, muslin and lining along the outside of the stitched line.

NOTE

Though a seam allowance is unnecessary when using a binding finish, some dress patterns require a seam allowance on the bodice. If required, leave the necessary amount of fabric intact outside the pencilled line when cutting away excess (fig. 2).

10. Attach binding in a contrasting colour along the edge of the collar, sleeves and/or skirt of the dress if the pattern requires binding.

11. Follow the instructions on the dress pattern for making up and finishing the dress.

Alice band and porcelain doll
Create a wonderfully co-ordinated outfit by adding an Alice band and satin ballet shoes (or even canvas shoes) decorated with satin ribbon roses to the *Bridesmaid's dress.*

Using the photographs of the Alice band (*see* this page and page 62) as a guide, make a few satin ribbon roses following the instructions given on pages 22–24. Sew or glue the roses to the Alice band and to some satin ballet shoes where appropriate (*see* photograph, below). A beautifully dressed porcelain doll (*see* this page) also offers a wonderful opportunity for using ribbon embroidery and satin ribbon roses, and makes a lovely gift.

SATIN RIBBON ROSES ARE HIGHLY EFFECTIVE FOR DECORATING BALLET SHOES, A PORCELAIN DOLL'S CLOTHING OR AN ALICE BAND

HARMONY
make one normal copy

X = ribbon roses: colour
    indicated at the X
G = green
P = pink
W = white
B = blue
Y = yellow
LP = light pink
DP = dark pink
A = apricot
• = B knots in
    two strands
○ = P knots
    in two
    strands
○ on leaves = W
    in two
    strands

P stem stitch
in two strands

G knot
in one
strand

G stem
stitch

G couching
in six strands

G couching

fill in with G couching

for tendrils
between leaves
use one strand
G stem stitch

G knots in one strand

stem stitch in two strands
for larger leaf shapes

stem stitch in
one strand.

bow is made in P stem stitch in two strands
fill up tie of bow with close-fitting knots in
two strands

THIS DESIGN IS ALSO SUITABLE FOR:
Shadow embroidery
Quilting/embroidery combinations

BORDEAUX
make one normal copy

G knots in two strands

G knots

DP stem stitch or backstitch

RP

RP backstitch

DP stem stitch or backstitch

DP

DP

G

G

LP

1

beads and RP knots in centre

RP for detail

DP couching in six strands

DP couching

G

P

G

X

P

P

G

A

P

17

18

P

G

DP

G

RP

G

RP

LP

A

16

15

RP for detail

A

B

2

Bead or DP

G

DP

bead or DP

beads and RP knots in centre

RP for detail

8

beads and RP knots in centre

Bead or DP

G

DP

LP

LP

A

G

G

14

7

RP for detail

C

G

DP

A

G

G

A

13

P

X

P

DP

DP

9

A

beads or DP

3

A

G

G

A

G

DP

G

DP

12

P

bead or DP

P

DP couching

DP

4

G

G

DP

10

DP

P

6

G

G

DP couching

X

G

DP stem stitch or backstitch

11

beads or DP

G

G

G

5

DP

DP couching

RP

beads or DP

G

A

A

G

G

A

G

G

G

RP

A

G

DP

RP

• = cream or green bead

X = dusty pink ribbon rose

DP stem stitch or backstitch

G

G

G

THIS DESIGN IS ALSO SUITABLE FO
Shadow embroidery
Quilting/embroidery combination

DP

ANTOINETTE 1

make one normal copy and join to
ANTOINETTE 2

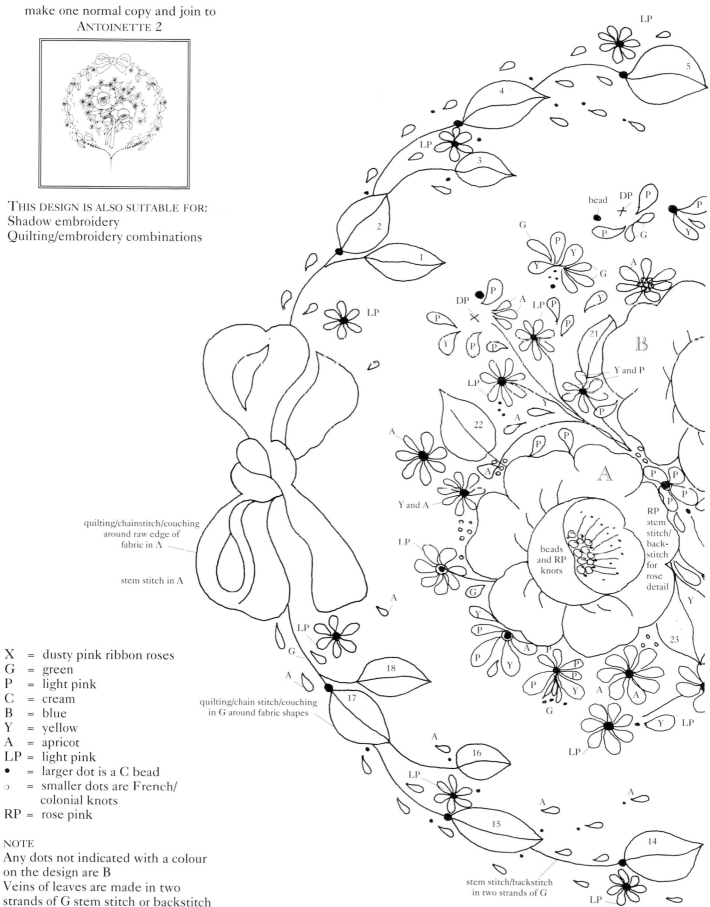

THIS DESIGN IS ALSO SUITABLE FOR:
Shadow embroidery
Quilting/embroidery combinations

quilting/chainstitch/couching
around raw edge of
fabric in A

stem stitch in A

bead

beads
and RP
knots

RP
stem
stitch/
back-
stitch
for
rose
detail

Y and P

Y and A

quilting/chain stitch/couching
in G around fabric shapes

stem stitch/backstitch
in two strands of G

X = dusty pink ribbon roses
G = green
P = light pink
C = cream
B = blue
Y = yellow
A = apricot
LP = light pink
• = larger dot is a C bead
○ = smaller dots are French/
      colonial knots
RP = rose pink

NOTE
Any dots not indicated with a colour
on the design are B
Veins of leaves are made in two
strands of G stem stitch or backstitch

ANTOINETTE 2
make one normal copy and join to ANTOINETTE 1

X = dusty pink ribbon roses
G = green
P = light pink
W = white
B = blue
Y = yellow
LP = light pink
RP = rose pink
A = apricot
C = cream
• = larger dot is a C bead
○ = smaller dots are French/colonial knots

NOTE
Any dots not indicated with a colour on the design are B
Veins on leaves are made in two strands of G stem stitch or backstitch

to make knots smaller, wind two strands three times around needle, then twice, and only once for the smallest knots

make one dot G and the following A, alternating the colours

two knots (one A, one G)

green couching – fill in

green couching

knots close together in two strands of G and A alternating for one flower

R A P T U R E 1

make one normal copy and join to RAPTURE 2

THIS DESIGN IS ALSO SUITABLE FOR:
Shadow embroidery
Quilting
Candlewicking

X = pink ribbon roses
G = green
P = pink
RP = rose pink
B = blue
Y = yellow
LP = light pink
C = cream
A = apricot
DP = dusty pink

NOTE
A C bead is sewn in the centre
of each lazy daisy and indicated
on this pattern with a large •
Any dots not coloured in this
design are B
Veins of leaves are made in two
strands of G stem stitch or
backstitch

G chainstitch
in one strand

DP stem stitch
in two strands

LP stem stitch
in two strands

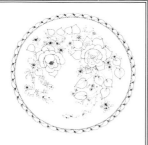

chainstitch or quilt around
raw edge of fabric leaves in G

RAPTURE 2
make one normal copy and join to
RAPTURE 1

THIS DESIGN IS ALSO SUITABLE FOR:
Shadow embroidery
Quilting
Candlewicking

X = pink ribbon roses
G = green
P = pink
RP = rose pink
B = blue
Y = yellow
LP = light pink
C = cream
A = apricot
DP = dusty pink

TRAVIATA 1
make one normal copy and
join to TRAVIATA 2

THIS DESIGN IS ALSO SUITABLE FOR:
Shadow embroidery
Candlewicking

X = pink ribbon roses
G = green
P = pink silk
W = white
B = blue
Y = yellow
DP = dusty pink
RP = rose pink
L = lilac
A = apricot
AB = aqua blue

NOTE
Any dot not indicated with
a colour is L

HINT
Add Y bead to centre
of ribbon rose after
attaching rose to
background

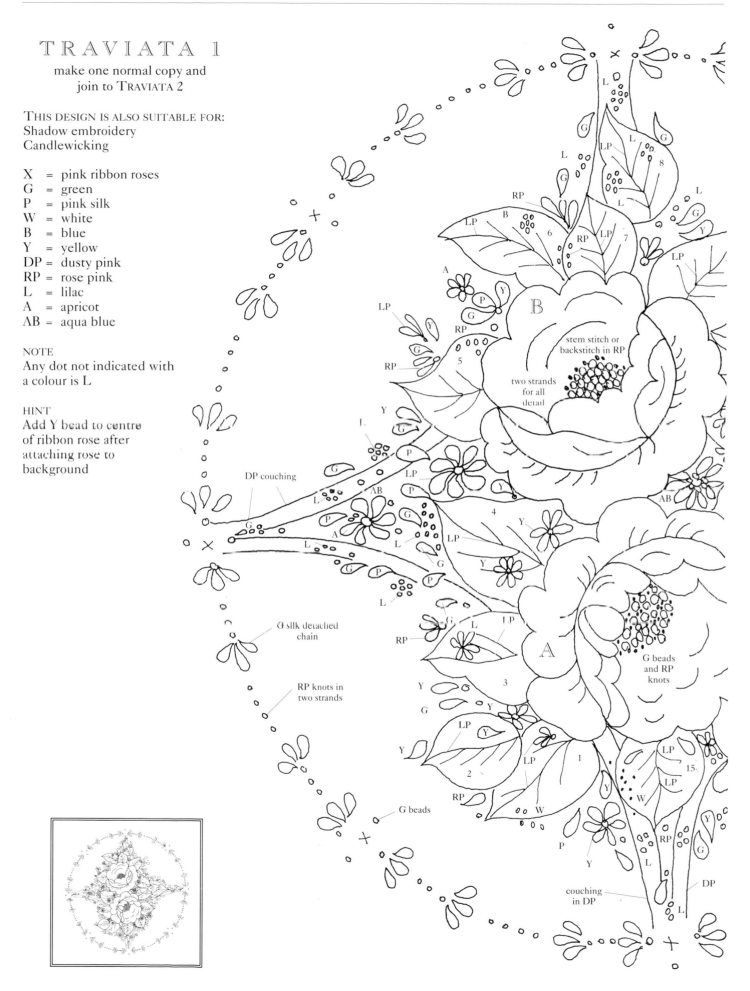

W G
9
L
G
Y
Y L
L P L
L Y G Y
P G
P G
10
Y
RP
P P 11
LP
L DP
L
L
couching in DP
X
L
12 P Y
Y
P G G
P G
P G
13 G

W
A
L Y
LP 14 G
P

Y G
'O L

G beads surrounding
P ribbon rose

G silk X

RP knots in
two strands

TRAVIATA 2
make one normal copy join to
TRAVIATA 1

THIS DESIGN IS ALSO SUITABLE FOR:
Shadow embroidery
Candlewicking

X = pink ribbon roses
G = green
P = pink silk
W = white
B = blue
Y = yellow
DP = dusty pink
RP = rose pink
L = lilac
A = apricot
AB = aqua blue

NOTE
Any dot not indicated with a
colour is L

HINT
Add Y bead to centre
of ribbon rose after
attaching rose to
background

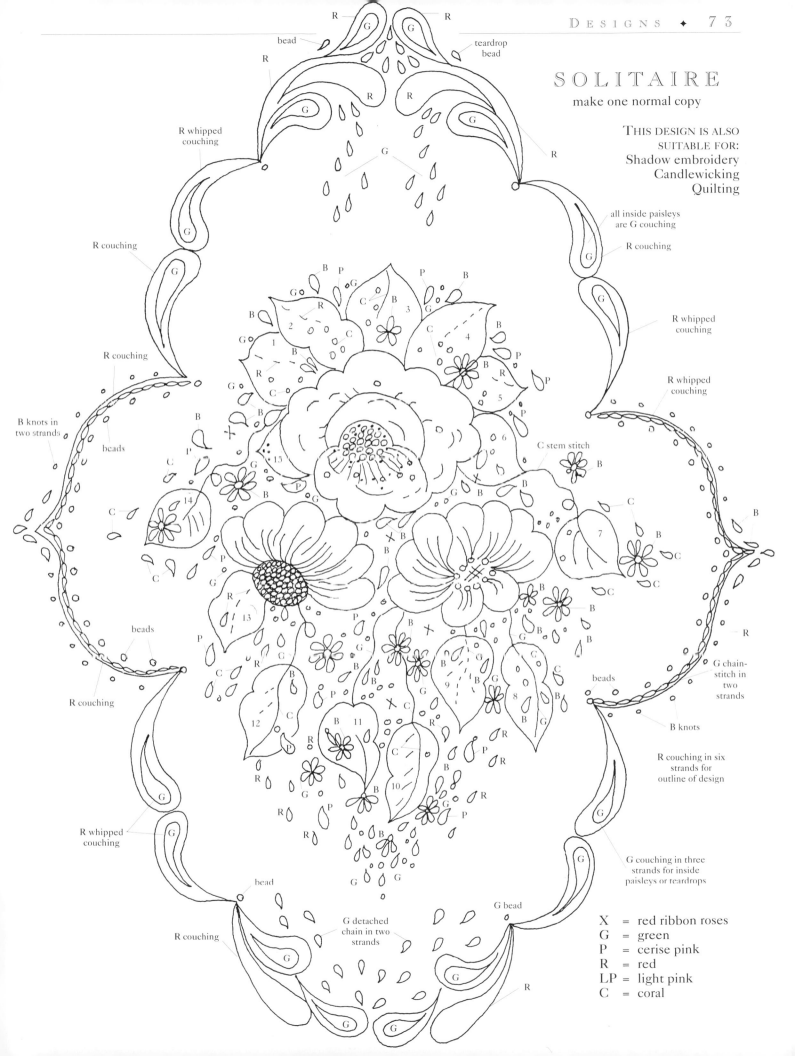

SOLITAIRE
make one normal copy

THIS DESIGN IS ALSO
SUITABLE FOR:
Shadow embroidery
Candlewicking
Quilting

all inside paisleys
are G couching

bead
teardrop
bead

R whipped
couching

R couching

R couching

R whipped
couching

R whipped
couching

R couching

B knots in
two strands

beads

C stem stitch

beads

G chain-
stitch in
two
strands

B knots

R couching in six
strands for
outline of design

R couching

beads

R whipped
couching

R couching

bead

G detached
chain in two
strands

G bead

G couching in three
strands for inside
paisleys or teardrops

X = red ribbon roses
G = green
P = cerise pink
R = red
LP = light pink
C = coral

ROSE CHAIN
make two normal copies and two reversed copies

SIZE: 41 x 41 cm (16 x 16 in)

THIS DESIGN IS ALSO SUITABLE FOR:
Quilting
Candlewicking
Machine appliqué
Shadow emboidery

HINT
Add B bead to centre of ribbon
rose after attaching rose

X = pink ribbon roses
G = green
P = pink
MP = medium pink
B = blue
Y = yellow
LP = light pink
DP = dark pink
C = cream

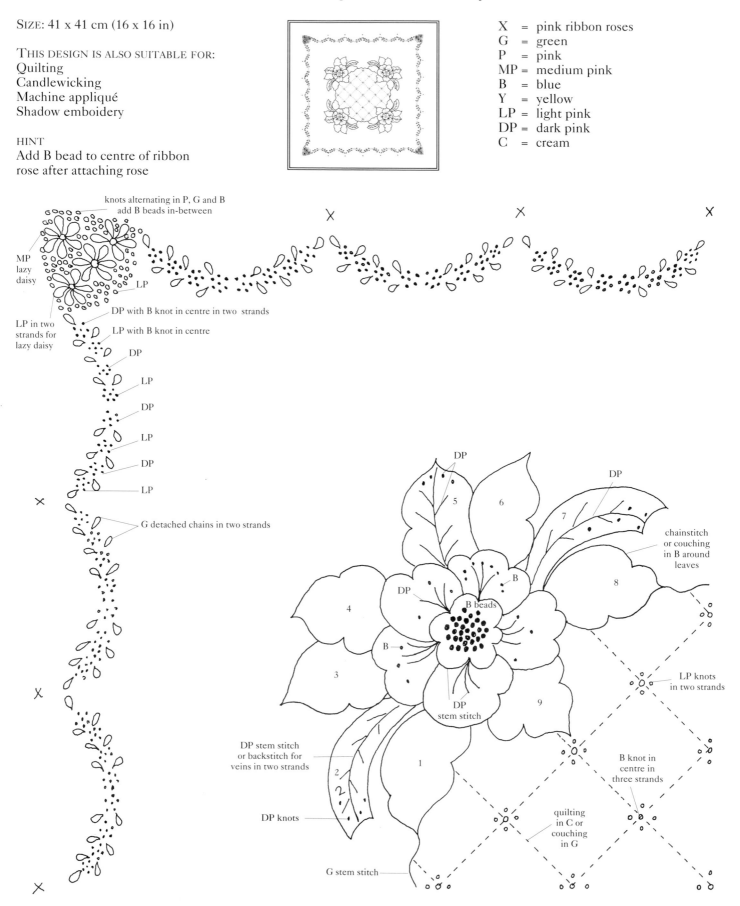

knots alternating in P, G and B
add B beads in-between

MP
lazy
daisy

LP

LP in two
strands for
lazy daisy

DP with B knot in centre in two strands

LP with B knot in centre

DP

LP

DP

LP

DP

LP

G detached chains in two strands

DP

DP

chainstitch
or couching
in B around
leaves

DP

B beads

B

DP
stem stitch

DP
stem stitch
or backstitch for
veins in two strands

DP knots

G stem stitch

LP knots
in two strands

B knot in
centre in
three strands

quilting
in C or
couching
in G

ODYSSEY

make two normal copies and two reversed copies

SIZE: 41 cm x 41 cm (16 in x 16 in)

THIS DESIGN IS ALSO SUITABLE FOR:
Shadow embroidery
Quilting
Candlewicking
Machine appliqué

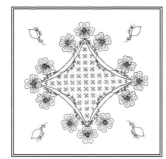

X = ribbon roses – colour
  indicated at the X
G = green
P = pink
DP = dusty pink
B = blue
Y = yellow
RP = rose pink
LP = light pink

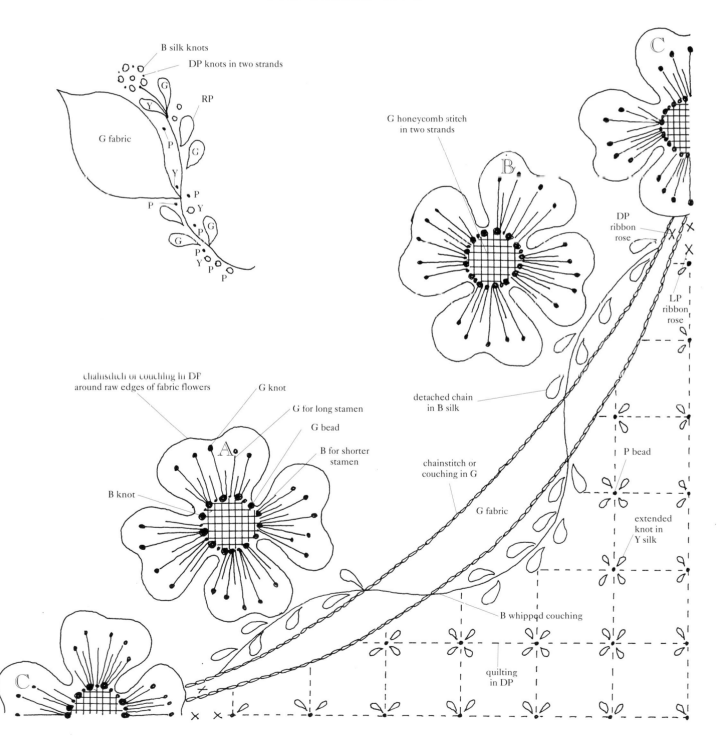

B silk knots
DP knots in two strands
G
Y
RP
G fabric
P
G
Y
P
P
Y
G
P
G
P
Y
P
P

G honeycomb stitch
in two strands

DP
ribbon
rose

LP
ribbon
rose

detached chain
in B silk

chainstitch or couching in DP
around raw edges of fabric flowers

G knot

G for long stamen

G bead

B for shorter
stamen

B knot

chainstitch or
couching in G

G fabric

P bead

extended
knot in
Y silk

B whipped couching

quilting
in DP

MONARCH
make two normal copies and two reversed copies

SIZE: 41 cm x 41 cm (16 in x 16 in)

THIS DESIGN IS ALSO SUITABLE FOR:
Candlewicking
Quilting
Shadow Embroidery

X = ribbon roses
G = green
P = pink
RP = rose pink
Y = yellow
L = lilac
DP = dusty pink
DG = darker green

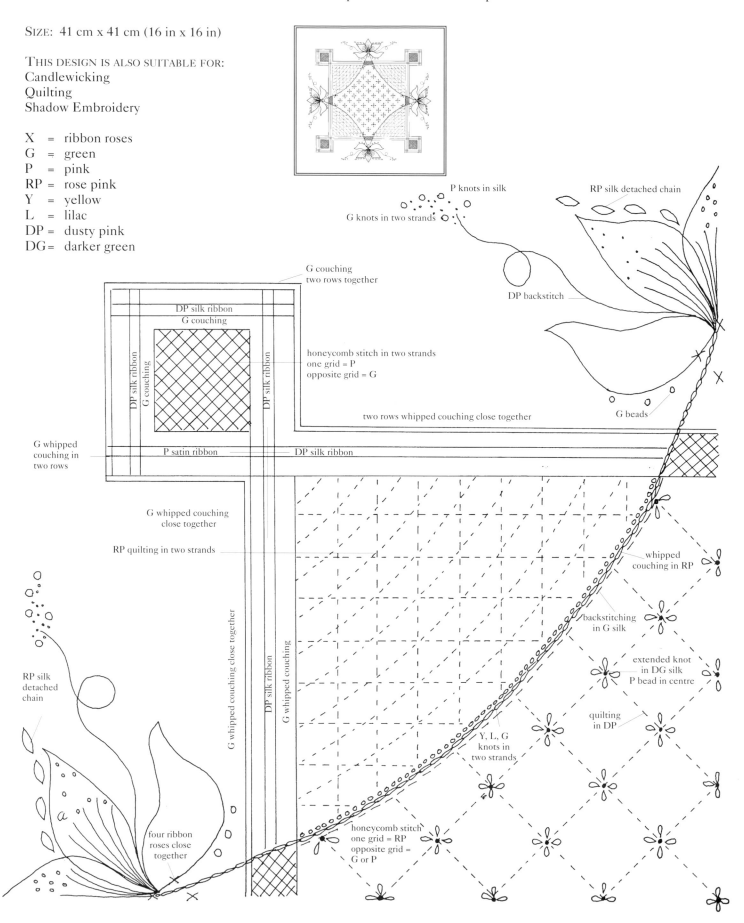

P knots in silk

G knots in two strands

RP silk detached chain

DP backstitch

G beads

G couching
two rows together

DP silk ribbon
G couching

DP silk ribbon

DP silk ribbon

G couching

honeycomb stitch in two strands
one grid = P
opposite grid = G

two rows whipped couching close together

G whipped
couching in
two rows

P satin ribbon

DP silk ribbon

G whipped couching
close together

RP quilting in two strands

whipped couching in RP

backstitching in G silk

extended knot in DG silk P bead in centre

quilting in DP

RP silk detached chain

G whipped couching close together

DP silk ribbon

G whipped couching

Y, L, G knots in two strands

four ribbon roses close together

honeycomb stitch one grid = RP opposite grid = G or P

RIBBONS AND BOWS
make two normal copies and two reversed copies

SIZE: 41 cm x 41 cm (16 in x 16 in)

THIS DESIGN IS ALSO SUITABLE FOR:
Candlewicking
Quilting
Machine appliqué
Shadow embroidery

G = green
P = pink
RP = rose pink
DP = dusty pink
X = ribbon roses

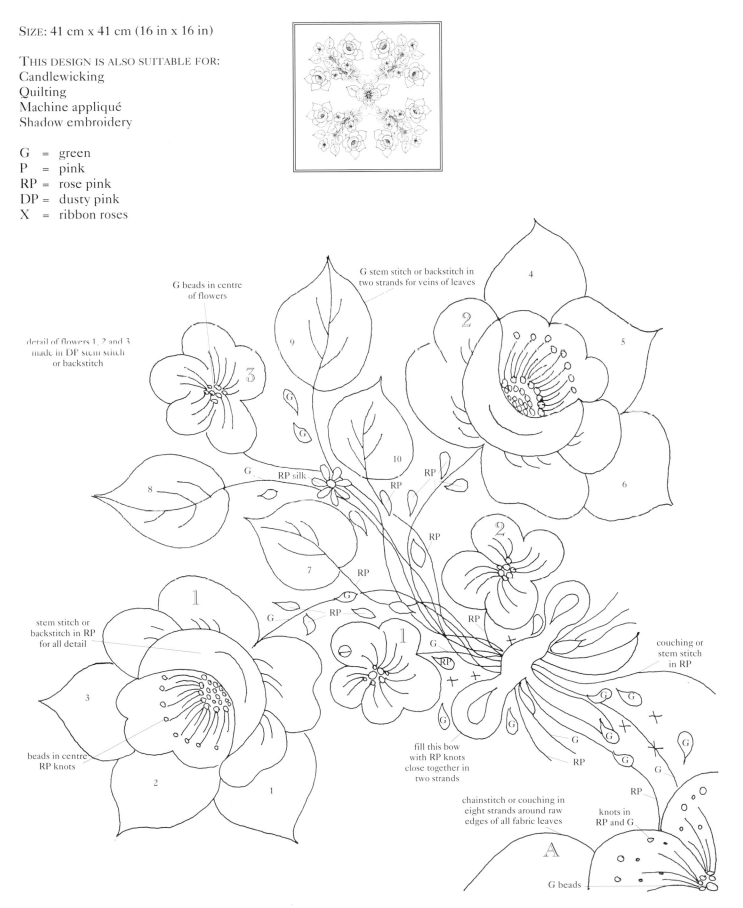

G beads in centre
of flowers

G stem stitch or backstitch in
two strands for veins of leaves

detail of flowers 1, 2 and 3
made in DP stem stitch
or backstitch

RP silk

stem stitch or
backstitch in RP
for all detail

beads in centre
RP knots

fill this bow
with RP knots
close together in
two strands

couching or
stem stitch
in RP

chainstitch or couching in
eight strands around raw
edges of all fabric leaves

knots in
RP and G

G beads

CAMROSE
make two normal copies and two
reversed copies

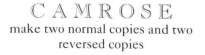

G = green
RP = RP
DP = DP
X = ribbon roses
A = apricot
DA = darker apricot
LA = lighter apricot
C = cream

THIS DESIGN IS ALSO SUITABLE FOR:
Candlewicking
Quilting
Machine appliqué
Shadow embroidery

bead or G
DA ribbon roses
RP
G
1
A in two strands
C
2
beads
3
couching
in DP
G silk
LA
G bead
quilting in C
4
5
G
B
RP
G
9
6
RP
G
7
A
8
G
DP stem stitch
or couching
DP   G

FILIGREE 1

make one normal copy and join to
FILIGREE 2

SIZE: 30 cm x 30 cm (12 in x 12 in)

G   = green
RP = rose pink
DP = dusty pink
P   = pink
B   = blue
Y   = yellow
T   = turquoise
L   = lavender

one large
backstitch
in DP

one large
backstitch
in B

knots in two
strands of Y,
B, L, G, P
and T

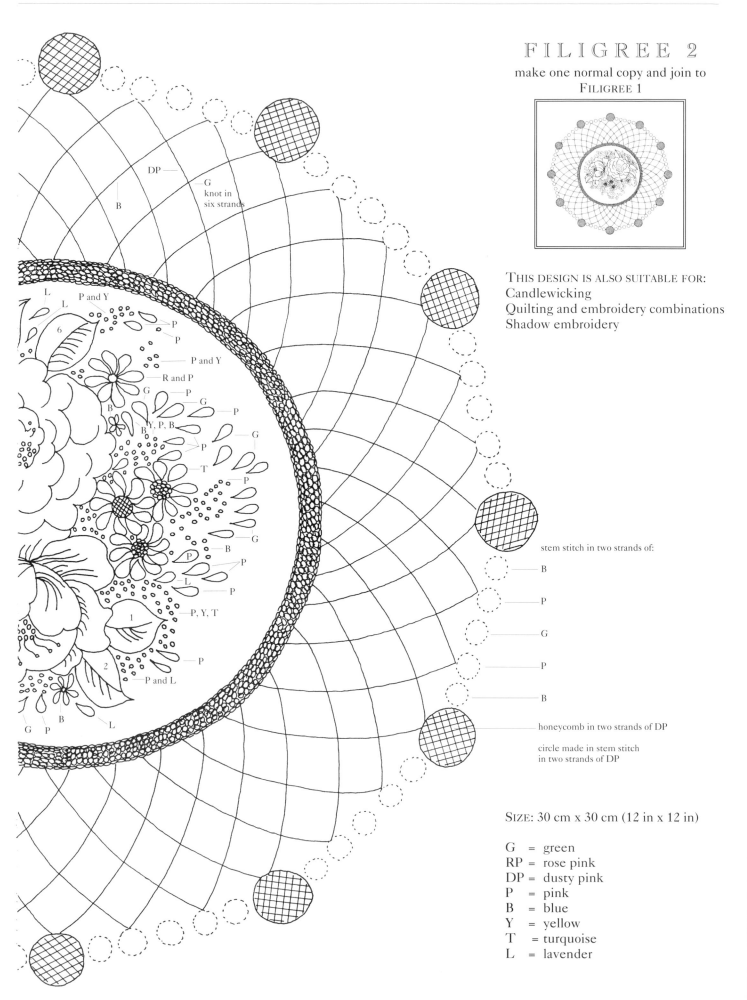

F I L I G R E E   2

make one normal copy and join to
F I L I G R E E   1

THIS DESIGN IS ALSO SUITABLE FOR:
Candlewicking
Quilting and embroidery combinations
Shadow embroidery

DP

G
knot in
six strands

B

L

L

P and Y

6

P

P

P and Y

R and P

G

P

G

P

B

Y, P, B

P

G

T

P

G

B

1

P

B

P

L

P

P, Y, T

2

P

P and L

G   P   B   L

stem stitch in two strands of:

B

P

G

P

B

honeycomb in two strands of DP

circle made in stem stitch
in two strands of DP

SIZE: 30 cm x 30 cm (12 in x 12 in)

G   = green
RP = rose pink
DP = dusty pink
P   = pink
B   = blue
Y   = yellow
T   = turquoise
L   = lavender

VICTORIAN TRELLIS
make two normal copies and two reversed copies

SIZE: 41 cm x 41 cm (16 in x 16 in)

G = green
DP = dusty pink
LP = light pink
B = blue
A = apricot
L = lavender

THIS DESIGN IS ALSO SUITABLE FOR:
Candlewicking
Quilting
Machine appliqué
Shadow embroidery

ACANTHUS

make two normal copies and
two reversed copies

THIS DESIGN IS ALSO SUITABLE FOR:
Candlewicking
Quilting
Shadow embroidery

SIZE: 41 cm x 41 cm (16 in x 16 in)

G = green
DP = dusty pink
LP = light pink
B = blue
A = apricot
L = lavender

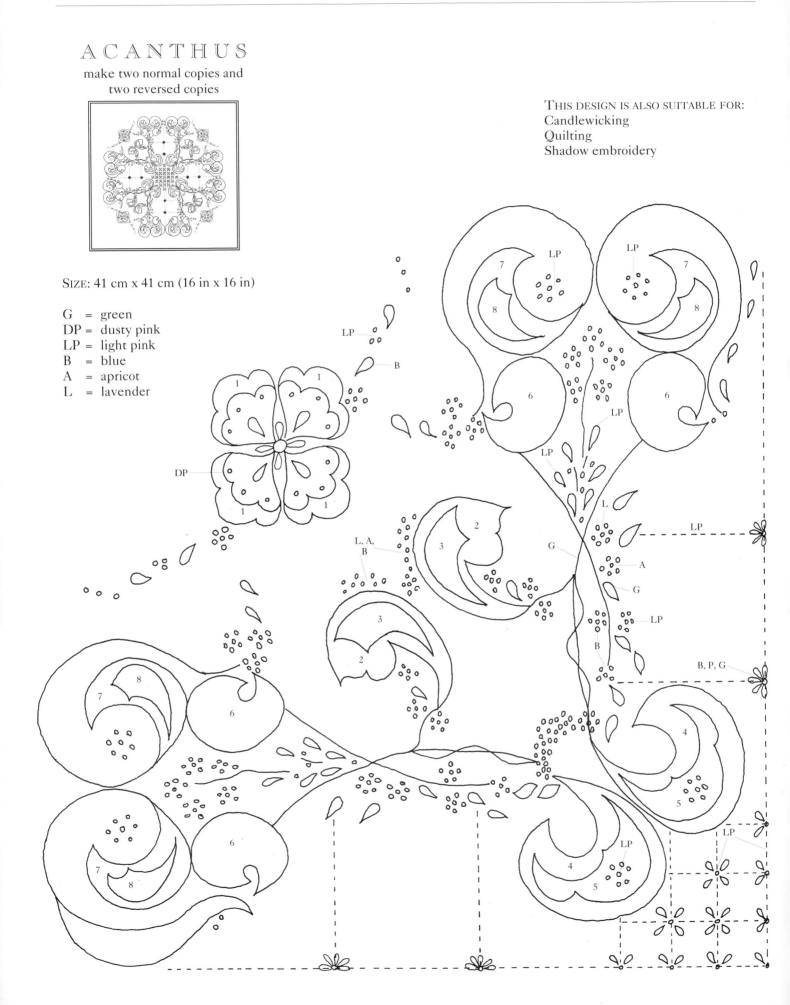

BYZANTINE
make two normal copies and two reversed copies

SIZE: 41 cm x 41 cm (16 in x 16 in)

G = green
DP = dusty pink
LP = lighter pink
B = blue
L = lavender
P = pink

THIS DESIGN IS ALSO SUITABLE FOR:
Candlewicking
Quilting
Shadow embroidery

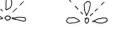

POMPEII
make two normal copies and
two reversed copies

SIZE: 41 cm x 41 cm (16 in x 16 in)

G   = green
DP = dusty pink
LP = lighter pink
B   = blue
P   = pink
L   = lavender

THIS DESIGN IS ALSO SUITABLE FOR:
Candlewicking
Quilting
Shadow embroidery

LP, G and B
silk knots

quilting in LP

LP, G, B

extended knot
in LP

G bead in
the centre

TEGAN-L

make two normal copies and two reversed copies

SIZE: 30 cm x 30 cm (12 in x 12 in)

G = green
LP = lighter pink
DP = dusty pink
RP = rose pink

THIS DESIGN IS ALSO SUITABLE FOR:
Candlewicking
Quilting
Shadow embroidery

FABRIC ROSE DETAIL: Use RP backstitch or stem stitch in one strand
FABRIC ROSE CENTRE: Use G beads
and RP knots
SHAPES 1 AND 13: Use G backstitch
or stem stitch in one strand
TEARDROP SHAPES ON G FABRIC
LEAVES: Use LP silk in detached
chain
FABRIC LEAVES: Use backstitch or
stem stitch in two strands for veins
STEMS OF LEAVES: Use backstitch
in two strands
CENTRE QUILTED CIRCLE: Use two
strands LP to quilt
Add extended French knots in LP and
at quilted intersections

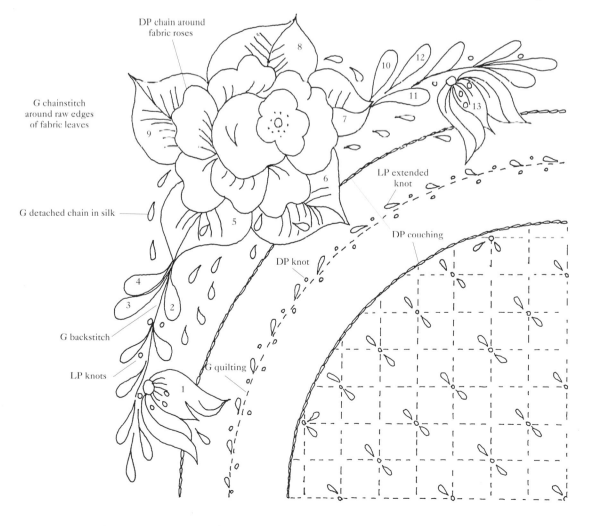

D A L E - L

make two normal copies and two reversed copies

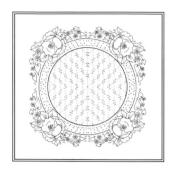

SIZE: 30 cm x 30 cm (12 in x 12 in)

G = green
LP = light pink
DP = dusty pink
RP = rose pink

FABRIC ROSE DETAIL: Use RP backstitch or stem stitch in one strand
FABRIC ROSE CENTRE: Use G beads
   and RP knots
DAISIES: Use LP silk, and a G bead
   in the centre of the daisy
LEAVES: Use G backstitch or stem
   stitch in two strands
STEMS: Use G backstitch in two
   strands
CENTRE CIRCLE: Quilted blocks –
   quilt in two strands of LP
Add silk knots in LP at the quilted
   intersections

THIS DESIGN IS ALSO SUITABLE FOR:
Candlewicking
Quilting
Shadow embroidery

Use the rose in this design for
machine appliqué onto tray-cloths,
placemats and napkins.

DP chainstitch around raw
   edge of fabric rose

G chainstitch around raw
   edge of fabric leaf

G backstitch

LP silk lazy daisy

G silk detached chain

DP couching

G and LP knots

G knot

G quilting

DP couching

SARAH-LEE

make two normal copies and two reversed copies

SIZE: 30 cm x 30 cm (12 in x12 in)

G = green
LP = light pink
DP = dusty pink
RP = rose pink

FABRIC ROSE DETAIL: Use RP backstitch in one strand for stamens and RP knots at the end of stamens. RP backstitch for other detail on rose. Add G beads to centre of rose and RP knots in-between.

FABRIC: Veins of leaves are made in two strands of stem stitch, or G backstitch

STEMS OF LEAVES: Use G backstitch in two strands

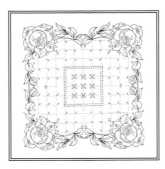

QUILTED BLOCKS: Use two strands LP. Add extended French knots in LP silk to form teardrop shapes at each intersection.

INSIDE SQUARE: French/colonial knots in LP, G and RP. Alternate the colours. LP silk to form daisies. Add a bead to the centre of the daisy.

THIS DESIGN IS ALSO SUITABLE FOR:
Candlewicking
Quilting
Shadow embroidery
Machine appliqué

LAUREN-JANE
make two normal copies and two reversed copies

SIZE: 30 cm x 30 cm (12 in x12 in)

G = green
LP = light pink
DP = dusty pink
RP = rose pink

THIS DESIGN IS ALSO SUITABLE FOR:
Candlewicking
Quilting
Shadow embroidery
Machine appliqué

Use sections of the design for adorning clothing and tray-cloths.

FABRIC ROSE DETAIL: Use RP back-stitch in one strand for stamens and other detail. Add G beads and RP knots to centre of rose.

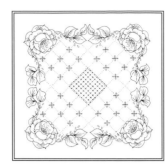

FABRIC LEAVES: Veins of leaves are made in two strands of stem stitch, or backstitch
STEMS OF LEAVES: Use two strands of G backstitch
QUILTED BLOCKS: Use two strands of LP silk. Add extended French knots in LP silk at intersections of quilted blocks.
INSIDE SQUARE: Use RP, G and LP knots in two strands. Alternate colours.
SMALL QUILTED INTERSECTIONS INSIDE SQUARE: LP silk knot at each dot

DP chainstitch around raw edge of fabric rose

LP knots in silk

G backstitch

G chainstitch around raw edge of fabric leaves

JASON-V
make two normal copies and two reversed copies

SIZE: 30 cm x 30 cm (12 in x12 in)

G = green
LP = light pink
DP = dusty pink
RP = rose pink

THIS DESIGN IS ALSO SUITABLE FOR:
Candlewicking
Quilting
Shadow embroidery
Machine appliqué

Use sections of the design for
adorning clothing and tray-cloths.

FABRIC ROSE DETAIL: Use RP backstitch in one strand
FABRIC ROSE CENTRES: Use RP backstitch for stamens and RP knots
in one strand for dots
FABRIC LEAVES: Use backstitch or
stem stitch in two strands for
veins of leaves
DAISIES: Use lazy daisy stitch in
LP silk, add G bead to centre
of daisies

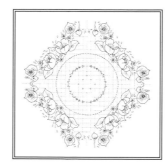

DAISIES ON LEAF 2: Lazy daisy
stitch in LP, and RP knots for
daisy centre
STEMS OF LEAVES: Use G backstitch
in two strands
OUTER CIRCLE: Quilt in DP in two
strands. Add knots in LP.
INNER CIRCLE: G detached chain in
two strands. DP knots for dots.
QUILTED BLOCKS: Use two strands
in LP
DOTS ON INSIDE CIRCLE SQUARES:
Knots in LP silk

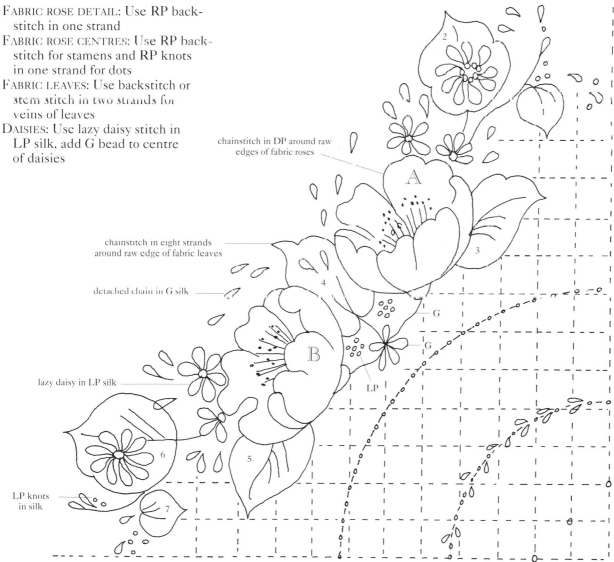

chainstitch in DP around raw
edges of fabric roses

chainstitch in eight strands
around raw edge of fabric leaves

detached chain in G silk

lazy daisy in LP silk

LP knots
in silk

GUYLIN-V

make two normal copies and two reversed copies

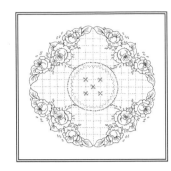

Size: 30 cm x 30 cm (12 in x12 in)

G   = green
LP = light pink
DP = dusty pink
RP = rose pink

This design is also suitable for:
Candlewicking
Quilting
Shadow embroidery

Fabric rose detail: Use RP
  backstitch in one strand for
  all three roses
Fabric rose centre: Use G beads
  and RP knots
Fabric leaves: Use backstitch or
  stem stitch in two strands for
  veins of leaves
Circular shape in centre: Use
  two strands in G detached chain
  for teardrop shapes and two strands
  in DP knots for dots
Dots inside circle: Use G, LP
  and RP knots in one strand and
  alternate colours
Teardrop shapes inside circle
  on intersections of quilted
  blocks: Use extended knots
  in LP silk
Quilted blocks: Use LP quilting
  in two strands

DP chainstitch around raw
edge of fabric roses

all teardrops
are G silk

chainstitch in G
around raw edge of
fabric leaves

PRINCESS

G   = green
LP = light pink
DP = dusty pink or peach
RP = rose pink
B   = blue
L   = lavender
Y   = yellow
LP = light pink
X   = satin ribbon roses
○   = French or colonial knots –
       use G, Y, B, LP, DP and L
℧○ in centre of roses = B beads
       or knots
Petal detail – use DP
Teardrop shapes = detached chain

THIS DESIGN IS ALSO SUITABLE FOR:
Embroidery
Appliqué by hand
Shadow embroidery
Quilting on clothing, tissue box
       covers, placemats, tray-cloths,
       napkins, tablecloths, toaster
       covers, tea cosies

ENLARGE FOR BIGGER PROJECTS

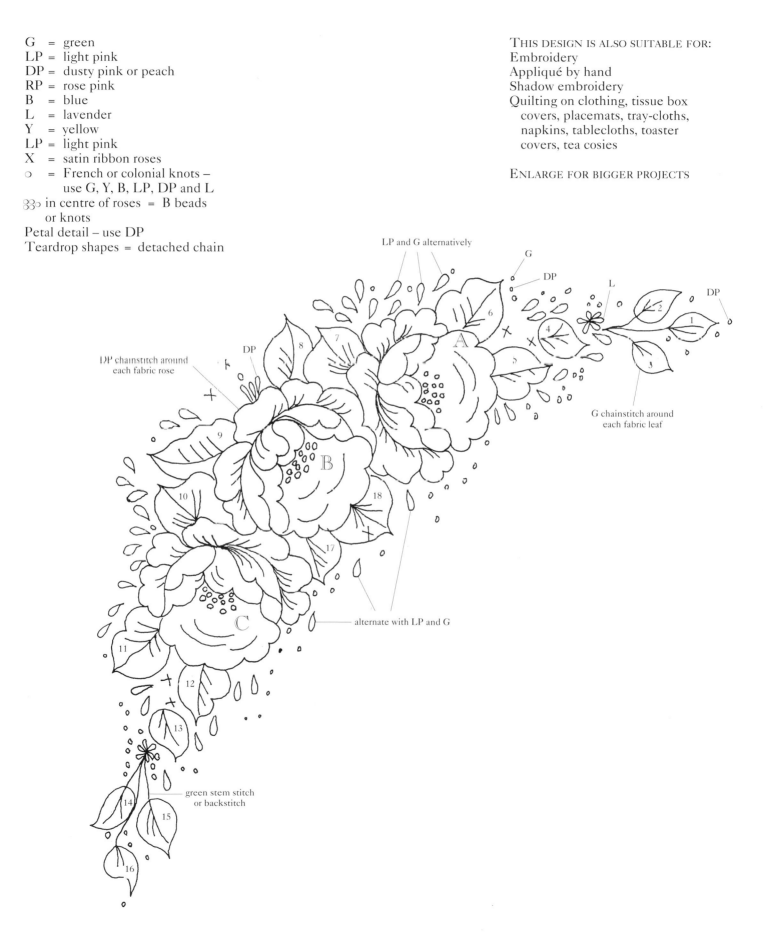

PETIT

ROSA

SNOWDROP

MISTY

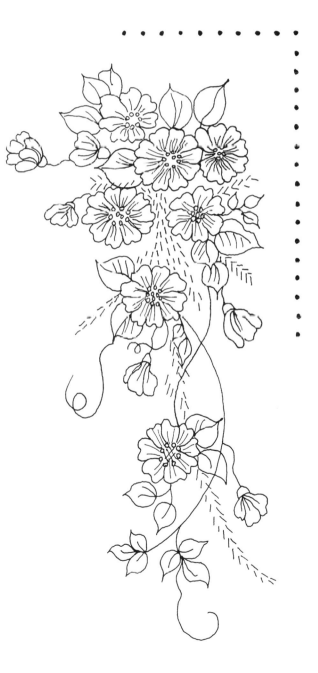

CAMELOT

FAERIE

If you experience any difficulty in obtaining the materials you require from local craft shops or department stores, the following addresses will be of help (alphabetical):

AUSTRALIA

Boronia Arts & Crafts Centre
247 Dorset Road
Boronia
Victoria 3155
Tel: (03) 762 1751

Burwood Craft Centre
173 Burwood Road
Burwood NSW 2134
Tel: (02) 747 5714

Gwen's Timeless Crafts
133 Unley Road
Unley
South Australia 5061
Tel: (08) 373 5271

Lincraft
Gallery Level, Imperial Arcade
Pitt Street
Sydney NSW 2000
Tel: (02) 221 5111

For other branches contact:
Lincraft Head Office
103 Stanley Street
West Melbourne
Victoria 3003
Tel: (03) 762 1751

Sundale Handcrafts
Shop 11 Logan Hyperdome
Pacific Highway
Loganholme
Queensland 4129
Tel: (07) 801 1121

NEW ZEALAND

Foote Brothers Ltd
43 Normanby Road
Mt Eden, Auckland
(Ribbon specialists/haberdashery)
Tel: (09) 623 4483

Jonora Needlecraft
Heard Park Shops
170 Parnell Road
Parnell
Auckland
(Needlecraft retailer)
Tel: (09) 379 7733

Manukau Sewing Centre
Shop 19 Manukau City
Shopping Centre
Manukau City
(Ribbon specialists/haberdashery)
Tel: (09) 262 1757

Needle Art 'n Craft
124 Great South Road
Papatoetoe
(Needlecraft retailer)
Tel: (09) 278 4345

Pinpoint Needlework Specialists
Selwyn Arcade
Great South Road
Papakura
(Needlecraft retailer)
Tel: (09) 298 4590

Sullivans
28 Sir William Avenue
East Tamaki
(Ribbon specialists/haberdashery)
Tel: (09) 274 6872

SOUTH AFRICA

Bernina Sew & Knit
53 Sanlam Plaza
Maitland Street
Bloemfontein 9301
Tel: (051) 47 2851, 47 6555
Fax: (051) 47 2537

Bernina Sew & Knit
Southdale Shopping Centre
Southdale
Johannesburg 2091
Tel: (011) 433 3551

Castellano Beltrame (Pty) Ltd
60 Old Pretoria Road
Halfway House 1685, Midrand
(Cushion cord, tassles and
decorative trimmings)
Tel: (011) 315 5437
Fax: (011) 315 5391

Crafty Supplies
32 Main Road
Claremont 7700
Cape Town
(Also mail order)
Tel: (021) 61 0286
Fax: (021) 61 0308

Doreen's Work Basket
Shop 91A
Westgate Shopping Centre
Roodepoort 1724
Tel/Fax: (011) 764 5305

Fabric Library
Stand 105
Old Pretoria Road
Halfway House 1685, Midrand
(Wide range of beautiful fabrics)
Tel: (011) 805 4211
Fax: (011) 315 1068

Handicraft Designs
P O Box 447
Underberg 4590, Natal
(Mail order – complete craft
kits as well as a wide range
of general supplies)
Tel: (033) 701 1045
Fax: (033) 701 1296

Needlewoman
Sanlam Plaza
Charles Street
Bloemfontein 9301
Tel: (051) 48 8151

Pearls and Pincushions
5 Maytime Centre
Charles Way
Kloof 3610
(General supplies)
Tel: (031) 764 6290
Fax: (031) 764 6291

Pickles & Patchwork
97 Howard Centre
Pinelands 7405
Tel: (021) 531 0617
Fax: (021) 531 9440

Pied Piper
13 Kemsley Street
Central
Port Elizabeth 6001
Tel/Fax: (041) 52 3090

Umbilo Drapers
684 Umbilo Road
Durban 4001
(Importers from
the UK and USA)
Tel: (031) 25 7814

W. A. Textiles t/a Home Fabrics
Stand 60
Old Pretoria Road
Halfway House 1685
Midrand

Woolcraft and Hobby
270 Boom Street
Pietermaritzburg 3201
(General supplies)
Tel: (0331) 45 4051
Fax: (0331) 94 3792

UNITED KINGDOM

Creativity Needlecrafts
45–47 New Oxford Street
London WC1
(Specialist supplier of
embroidery, tapestry
and knitting materials –
mail order)
Tel: (0171) 240 2945

Fred Aldous Ltd
P O Box 135
37 Lever Street
Manchester 1
M60 1UX
(Suppliers of craft
materials – mail order)
Tel: (0161) 236 2477
Fax: (0161) 236 6075

John Lewis Partnership
278–306 Oxford Street
London W1A 6AH
(General)
Tel: (0171) 629 7711

Offray Ltd
Ashbury
Rosscrea
County Tipperary
Eire
(Specialist ribbon
manufacturer/supplier)
Tel: (0171) 631 3548

Specialist Crafts Ltd
P O Box 247
Leicester LE1 9QS
(Mail order)
Tel: (0116) 251 0405

V. V. Rouleaux
10 Symons Street
London SW3 2TJ
(Specialist ribbon suppliers)
Tel: (0171) 371 5929

W. Williams & Son Ltd
Regent House
1 Thane Villas
London N7
(Suppliers of ribbon – wholesale)
Tel: (0171) 263 7311

UNITED STATES

C. M. Offray & Son Inc
857 Willow Circle
Hagerstown
Maryland 21740
(Ribbon manufacturer)